Essentials of the California Verbal Learning Test

Essentials of Psychological Assessment Series

Series Editors, Alan S. Kaufman and Nadeen L. Kaufman

Essentials of 16PF® Assessment
by Heather E. P. Cattell and James M. Schuerger
Essentials of Adaptive Behavior Assessment of Neurodevelopmental Disorders
by Celine A. Saulnier and Cheryl Klaiman
Essentials of ADHD Assessment for Children and Adolescents
by Elizabeth P. Sparrow and Drew Erhardt
Essentials of Assessing, Preventing, and Overcoming Reading Difficulties
by David A. Kilpatrick
Essentials of Assessment Report Writing, Second Edition
by W. Joel Schneider, Elizabeth O. Lichtenberger, Nancy Mather, Nadeen L. Kaufman, and Alan S. Kaufman
Essentials of Assessment with Brief Intelligence Tests
by Susan R. Homack and Cecil R. Reynolds
Essentials of Autism Spectrum Disorders Evaluation and Assessment
by Celine A. Saulnier and Pamela E. Ventola
Essentials of Bayley Scales of Infant Development-II Assessment
by Maureen M. Black and Kathleen Matula
Essentials of Behavioral Assessment
by Michael C. Ramsay, Cecil R. Reynolds, and R. W. Kamphaus
Essentials of Career Interest Assessment
by Jeffrey P. Prince and Lisa J. Heiser
Essentials of CAS2 Assessment
by Jack A. Naglieri and Tulio M. Otero
Essentials of Child and Adolescent Psychopathology, Second Edition
by Linda Wilmshurst
Essentials of Cognitive Assessment with KAIT and Other Kaufman Measures
by Elizabeth O. Lichtenberger, Debra Y. Broadbooks, and Alan S. Kaufman
Essentials of Conners Behavior Assessments™
by Elizabeth P. Sparrow
Essentials of Creativity Assessment
by James C. Kaufman, Jonathan A. Plucker, and John Baer
Essentials of Cross-Battery Assessment, Third Edition
by Dawn P. Flanagan, Samuel O. Ortiz, and Vincent C. Alfonso
Essentials of DAS-II® Assessment
by Ron Dumont, John O. Willis, and Colin D. Elliott
Essentials of Dyslexia Assessment and Intervention
by Nancy Mather and Barbara J. Wendling
Essentials of Evidence-Based Academic Interventions
by Barbara J. Wendling and Nancy Mather
Essentials of Executive Functions Assessment
by George McCloskey and Lisa A. Perkins
Essentials of Forensic Psychological Assessment, Second Edition
by Marc J. Ackerman
Essentials of Gifted Assessment
by Steven I. Pfeiffer
Essentials of IDEA for Assessment Professionals
by Guy McBride, Ron Dumont, and John O. Willis
Essentials of Individual Achievement Assessment
by Douglas K. Smith
Essentials of Intellectual Disability Assessment and Identification
by Alan W. Brue and Linda Wilmshurst
Essentials of KABC-II Assessment
by Alan S. Kaufman, Elizabeth O. Lichtenberger, Elaine Fletcher-Janzen, and Nadeen L. Kaufman
Essentials of KTEA™-3 and WIAT®-III Assessment
by Kristina C. Breaux and Elizabeth O. Lichtenberger
Essentials of MCMI®-IV Assessment
by Seth D. Grossman and Blaise Amendolace
Essentials of Millon™ Inventories Assessment, Third Edition
by Stephen Strack
Essentials of MMPI-A™ Assessment
by Robert P. Archer and Radhika Krishnamurthy
Essentials of MMPI-2® Assessment, Second Edition
by David S. Nichols
Essentials of Myers-Briggs Type Indicator® Assessment, Second Edition
by Naomi L. Quenk
Essentials of NEPSY®-II Assessment
by Sally L. Kemp and Marit Korkman
Essentials of Nonverbal Assessment
by Steve McCallum, Bruce Bracken, and John Wasserman
Essentials of PAI® Assessment
by Leslie C. Morey
Essentials of Planning, Selecting, and Tailoring Interventions for Unique Learners
by Jennifer T. Mascolo, Vincent C. Alfonso, and Dawn P. Flanagan
Essentials of Processing Assessment, Third Edition
by Milton J. Dehn
Essentials of Psychological Assessment Supervision
by A. Jordan Wright
Essentials of Psychological Testing, Second Edition
by Susana Urbina
Essentials of Response to Intervention
by Amanda M. VanDerHeyden and Matthew K. Burns
Essentials of Rorschach® Assessment
by Tara Rose, Michael P. Maloney, and Nancy Kaser-Boyd
Essentials of Rorschach Assessment: Comprehensive System and R-PAS
by Jessica R. Gurley
Essentials of School Neuropsychological Assessment, Third Edition
by Daniel C. Miller and Denise E. Maricle
Essentials of Specific Learning Disability Identification, Second Edition
by Vincent C. Alfonso and Dawn P. Flanagan
Essentials of Stanford-Binet Intelligence Scales (SB5) Assessment
by Gale H. Roid and R. Andrew Barram
Essentials of TAT and Other Storytelling Assessments, Second Edition
by Hedwig Teglasi
Essentials of Temperament Assessment
by Diana Joyce
Essentials of Trauma-Informed Assessment and Interventions in School and Community Settings
by Kirby L. Wycoff and Bettina Franzese
Essentials of WAIS®-IV Assessment, Second Edition
by Elizabeth O. Lichtenberger and Alan S. Kaufman
Essentials of WISC®-IV Assessment, Second Edition
by Dawn P. Flanagan and Alan S. Kaufman
Essentials of WISC-V® Assessment
by Dawn P. Flanagan and Vincent C. Alfonso
Essentials of WISC-V Integrated Assessment
by Susan Engi Raiford
Essentials of WJ IV® Cognitive Abilities Assessment
by Fredrick A. Schrank, Scott L. Decker, and John M. Garruto
Essentials of WJ IV® Tests of Achievement
by Nancy Mather and Barbara J. Wendling
Essentials of WMS®-IV Assessment
by Lisa Whipple Drozdick, James A. Holdnack, and Robin C. Hilsabeck
Essentials of WNV™ Assessment
by Kimberly A. Brunnert, Jack A. Naglieri, and Steven T. Hardy-Braz
Essentials of Working Memory Assessment and Intervention
by Milton J. Dehn
Essentials of WPPSI™-IV Assessment
by Susan Engi Raiford and Diane L. Coalson
Essentials of WRAML2 and TOMAL-2 Assessment
by Wayne Adams and Cecil R. Reynolds
Essentials of Treatment Planning, Second Edition
by Mark E. Maruish
Essentials of the California Verbal Learning Test
by Thomas J. Farrer and Lisa Whipple Drozdick

Essentials

of the California Verbal Learning Test

CVLT-C, CVLT-II, & CVLT3

Edited by

Thomas J. Farrer

Lisa Whipple Drozdick

WILEY

This edition first published 2020

Registered Office
John Wiley & Sons, Inc., 111 River Street, Hoboken, NJ 07030, USA

Editorial Office
111 River Street, Hoboken, NJ 07030, USA

For details of our global editorial offices, customer services, and more information about Wiley products visit us at www.wiley.com.

Wiley also publishes its books in a variety of electronic formats and by print-on-demand. Some content that appears in standard print versions of this book may not be available in other formats.

Library of Congress Cataloging-in-Publication Data

Names: Farrer, Thomas J. (Thomas Jeffrey), 1983- editor. | Drozdick, Lisa Whipple, editor. | John Wiley & Sons.
Title: Essentials of the California Verbal Learning Test : CVLT-C, CVLT-2, & CVLT3 / edited by Thomas J Farrer & Lisa Drozdick. Other titles: Essentials of psychological assessment series.
Description: First Edition. | Hoboken : Wiley, 2020. | Series: Essentials of psychological assessment | Includes index.
Identifiers: LCCN 2019051999 (print) | LCCN 2019052000 (ebook) | ISBN 9781119578567 (Paperback) | ISBN 9781119578604 (Adobe PDF) | ISBN 9781119578451 (ePub)
Subjects: LCSH: Verbal learning—Testing—Handbooks, manuals, etc. | Memory—Testing—Handbooks, manuals, etc. | Neuropsychological tests—Handbooks, manuals, etc.
Classification: LCC LB1060 .E86 2020 (print) | LCC LB1060 (ebook) | DDC 370.15/23—dc23
LC record available at https://lccn.loc.gov/2019051999
LC ebook record available at https://lccn.loc.gov/2019052000

Cover Design: Wiley
Cover Image: © Greg Kuchik/Getty Images

Set in 9.5/11pt AGaramondPro by SPi Global, Chennai, India

MIX
Paper from responsible sources
FSC
www.fsc.org
FSC® C013604

CONTENTS

Essentials of the California Verbal Learning Test

One

OVERVIEW

INTRODUCTION

During development in childhood, verbal learning and memory are key to success in school and language acquisition and development. A large portion of time is spent in activities requiring retention of verbal information, such as conversations with parents and peers, reading, and interacting with digital devices. The ability to encode and retain verbal information remains elemental throughout the lifespan as much learning and social interaction requires adequate verbal learning and memory ability. Therefore, the assessment of verbal memory is an essential component of clinical and neuropsychological evaluations. This is particularly relevant for evaluations of individuals with known or suspected cognitive or language impairments. Many developmental, neurological, and psychiatric disorders involve disruption or impairment of memory processes (e.g., attention-deficit hyperactivity disorder, dementia, traumatic brain injury). Although some areas of memory decline normally with age (Salthouse, 1996; Tromp, Dufour, Lithfous, Pebayle, & Després, 2015), the prevalence of memory disorders increases with age and memory complaints are a frequent concern cited by older adults. Evaluation of memory processes can assist in differentiating normative development and decline across the lifespan from memory deficits related to insidious origins.

The California Verbal Learning Test, Third Edition (CVLT3; Delis, Kramer, Kaplan, & Ober, 2017) provides a detailed look into verbal learning and memory processes for individuals ages 16–90. It introduced some major scoring changes and updates from the CVLT, second edition (CVLT-II; Delis, Kramer, Kaplan, & Ober, 2000). However, since the CVLT-II is still widely used in clinical and research settings, both editions are described in this book. The CVLT children's version (CVLT-C; Delis, Kramer, Kaplan, & Ober, 1994) provides a similar assessment of memory for individuals ages 5–16. This book provides an easy-to-use reference for individuals learning the essentials of administration, scoring, and interpretation of the CVLT3, CVLT-II, or the CVLT-C. It maintains the direct, systematic approach to presenting material that is characteristic of the Essentials series. In addition, guidelines for selecting the best CVLT product for a specific client and administrative and interpretive guidelines are provided. The latest research on the CVLT products and on verbal memory processes is also included throughout the chapters to assist in applying results obtained with the most recent CVLT editions.

Essentials of California Verbal Learning Test: CVLT-C, CVLT-II, & CVLT3 covers topics that emphasize the appropriate administration, scoring, interpretation, and application of each test. Each chapter includes several "Rapid Reference," "Caution," or "Don't Forget" boxes to highlight important points for easy reference and clarification. At the end of each chapter, a short "Test Yourself" quiz is provided to help you solidify what you have read. The information in this book is provided to help you understand the nuances of each of the CVLT instruments and become a proficient user.

HISTORY AND DEVELOPMENT

Although the concept of investigating the processes underlying memory is standard in memory assessment instruments today, at the time the original CVLT (Delis, Kramer, Kaplan, & Ober, 1987) was developed in 1987 it was a novel approach to assessment. The authors combined research and clinical experience with patients with memory deficits to create a novel approach to assessing learning and memory processes. Memory deficits were linked to specific tasks within a 16-word memory recall and recognition test. The 16 words were derived from four semantic categories, allowing the examinee to group words semantically as an aid to recalling the words. This approach allows examination of not only how much an individual can learn and retain but also the strategies used to learn and recall information and the types of memory errors made. These additional measures provide detailed information on the processes involved in learning and memory to aid in diagnosis and intervention planning.

In the original CVLT, the examiner read a Monday shopping list that contained 16 items to the examinee. The 16 items consisted of four words from four different semantic categories (tools, fruit, clothing, spices, and herbs). The Monday shopping list was repeated in five learning trials, followed by an interference list trial. A Tuesday shopping interference list also comprised 16 words from four categories. Two of the categories overlapped with categories from the Monday list and two were novel categories. Following recall of the Tuesday list, the examinee was asked to recall the Monday list in both a free-recall and a cued-recall trial. During the cued-recall trial, the examiner provided each of the four semantic categories and asked the examinee to name the items from each. The examiner than waited 20 min before administering delayed free- and cued-recall trials, as well as a delayed recognition trial (see Figure 1.1). The examiner was encouraged to administer nonverbal tasks during this 20-min delay. Scores derived on the CVLT assessed attention, learning strategies, recall accuracy, interference effects, recall errors, and recognition. The original normative sample consisted of 273 neurologically intact individuals (104 males, 169 females) recruited from other research studies being conducted at the time of data collection.

Since 1987, three revisions and expansions of the CVLT have been published, although the administration has remained remarkably stable. The expansion and evolution of the CVLT reflect the growing influence and use of the process approach to memory assessment. Its wide use in research on memory also ensures several editions of the CVLT will remain in use for a long time. The currently available editions include the CVLT3 (published in 2017), the CVLT-II (published in 2000), and the CVLT-C (published in 1994). Each of the editions reflects the knowledge and theories of memory at the time of its development as well as the developmental needs of the population assessed. This chapter provides an overview of the content of each of the currently available CVLT instruments,

Learning trials	Interference trial	Short-delay	Long-delay (follows 20-min delay)	Yes/No recognition	Forced-choice recognition (follows 10-min delay)[a]
Trial 1 Free Recall	List B Free Recall	Short-Delay Free Recall	Long-Delay Free Recall	Yes/No Recognition	Forced-Choice Recognition
Trial 2 Free Recall		Short-Delay Cued Recall	Long-Delay Cued Recall		
Trial 3 Free Recall					
Trial 4 Free Recall					
Trial 5 Free Recall					

[a]Only on CVLT-II and CVLT3.

Figure 1.1. CVLT-C, CVLT-II standard and alternate, and CVLT3 standard and alternate forms structure.

and later chapters provide a review of the research literature related to memory and learning as measured by the CVLT.

OVERVIEW AND ORGANIZATION OF THE CVLT-C

The CVLT was expanded to younger ages with the publication of the CVLT-C. It not only extended the age downward to 5, it also modified the content to be more relevant for children. The word list was shortened to 15 words derived from three semantic categories. The semantic categories reflect categories common in childhood. Two of these categories overlap with the semantic categories contained in the adult forms. Similar to the administration of the original CVLT, the child is read the list of 15 words across five learning trials, followed by an interference list trial. Just as in the original CVLT, the lists are presented as Monday and Tuesday shopping lists. Following the interference trial, the child recalls the original list in both short-delay free- and cued-recall trials. The examiner then completes nonverbal testing for 20 min before administering long-delay free- and cued-recall trials, as well as a delayed recognition trial (see Figure 1.1). All trials are required to derive the primary scores. Scores derived on the CVLT-C assess auditory attention, learning strategies and characteristics, recall accuracy and consistency, proactive and retroactive interference, recall errors, and recognition.

A *T* score is derived for the learning trials (Trials 1–5 Total) with a mean of 50 and a standard deviation of 10. The process scores provided in the CVLT-C provide detailed information about the learning and memory processes required to recall verbal information. For these scores, age-corrected *z* scores are provided with a mean of 0 and a standard deviation of 1. The scores derived in CVLT-C are listed in Rapid Reference 1.1 by condition. Detailed information on calculating scores is provided in Chapter 3.

Rapid Reference 1.1

Primary Scores Derived in CVLT-C, by Condition

Learning trials	Recall scores	Recognition scores
Trial 1 Free-Recall Correct	Short-Delay Free Recall	Recognition Hits
Trial 5 Free-Recall Correct	Short-Delay Cued Recall	Discriminability
Total Trials 1–5 (*T* score)	Short-Delay Free Recall vs. List A Trial 5 (difference score)	Discriminability vs. Long-Delay Free Recall
List B Free-Recall Trial	Long-Delay Free Recall	False Positives
List B Recall vs. List A Trial 1 Recall (difference score)	Long-Delay Cued Recall	Response Bias
Semantic Cluster Ratio	Long-Delay Free Recall vs. Short-Delay Free Recall (difference score)	
Serial Cluster Ratio	Total Perseverations	
Expected Serial Clustering	Total Free-Recall Intrusions	
Percent of Total Recall from Primacy Region	Total Cued-Recall Intrusions	
Percent of Total Recall from Middle Region	Total Intrusions	
Percent of Total Recall from Recency Region		
Learning Slope		
Recall Consistency		

Difference scores compare performance on one task to performance on another task. On CVLT-C, difference scores are derived using two methods (see Chapter 3 for detailed information on calculating the change scores): raw percentage change and scaled score difference. The raw percentage change scores are not normed due to the heavy influence of the raw scores on the calculation of percentage retained, such that low overall recall can result in higher retention percentages. Difference (or savings) scores utilize the age-corrected scaled scores. Means and standard deviations for the normative sample are provided to provide context for these scores. Change and difference scores should not replace the primary scores but are used to guide the interpretation of differences observed across conditions. Detailed information on the interpretation of scores is provided in Chapter 4.

OVERVIEW AND ORGANIZATION OF THE CVLT-II

The CVLT-II was the first major revision to the CVLT. The revision was guided by neuropsychological and cognitive research on memory, feedback from users and reviewers of the CVLT (both personal and published), and clinical experience by the authors. One of the major criticisms of the CVLT was the small, nonrepresentative sample used for the norms. Multiple studies demonstrated that the norms resulted in lower than expected scores in individuals with average to low educational attainment (Paolo, Troster, & Ryan, 1997; Wiens, Tindall, & Crossen, 1994). A large representative sample of the population aged 16–89 was collected to update the norms across seven age bands. In terms of content, the 16 items used in the word lists were modified to be easier to understand and were not presented as a shopping list. The word lists were derived using high-frequency words commonly spoken within the United States from four different semantic categories. The interference list also comprised 16 words from four categories, two of which overlapped with the original list. In addition, a forced-choice recognition trial was added to assess insufficient effort. Two new forms were also introduced with the CVLT-II: an Alternate Form and a Short Form. The Alternate Form is equated to the Standard Form, utilizes the same administration format, and provides the same scores as the Standard Form but uses alternate word lists from the Standard Form. The Short Form uses a nine-word list with a shortened format to accommodate use as a screener or with individuals that cannot tolerate lengthy testing. The Standard and Alternate Forms take 30 min to administer (in addition to the 20-min delay and an optional 10-min delay to administer the forced-choice recognition condition), whereas the Short Form takes around 20 min (in addition to the 10-min delay).

The development of the CVLT-II incorporated analysis of the performance of each score to evaluate the influence of demographic variables and general cognitive ability on performance, reliability and stability, score range and distribution for floor and ceiling problems, and clinical utility. Norms are corrected for age and sex because these demographic factors contributed more than 5% of the variance in primary scores. Detailed information on the psychometric properties and the clinical utility of the CVLT-II are described in the *CVLT-II Manual* (Delis, Kramer, Kaplan, & Ober, 2000).

Just as on the original CVLT, for the Standard and Alternate Forms, the examinee is read a list of 16 words across five learning trials, followed by an interference list trial. Following the interference trial, the examinee recalls the original list in both free-recall and cued-recall trials. The examiner then completes nonverbal testing for 20 min before administering delayed free-recall and cued-recall trials, as well as a delayed yes/no recognition trial. The examiner may then administer an optional forced-choice recognition trial following a 10-min delay (see Figure 1.2). All trials except the forced-choice recognition trial are required to derive the primary scores. It is highly recommended that examiners routinely administer the forced-choice recognition condition to assess performance validity.

For the Short Form, the examinee is read a list of nine words (from three semantic categories) across four learning trials, followed by a 30-s distractor task. Following the distraction task, the examinee is asked to recall the list in a short-delay free-recall trial. The examiner than completes nonverbal testing for 10 min before administering long-delay free- and cued-recall trials, as well as a delayed yes/no recognition trial. The examiner may then administer an optional forced-choice recognition trial following a 5-min delay (see Figure 1.3). All trials except the forced-choice recognition trial are required to derive

Learning trials	30-second distractor task	Short-delay	Long-delay (follows 10-min delay)	Yes/No recognition	Forced-choice recognition (follows a 5-min delay)
Trial 1 Free Recall		Short-Delay Free Recall	Long-Delay Free Recall	Yes/No Recognition	Forced-Choice Recognition
Trial 2 Free Recall			Long-Delay Cued Recall		
Trial 3 Free Recall					
Trial 4 Free Recall					

Figure 1.2. CVLT-II and CVLT3 structure, brief form.

the primary scores. See Rapid Reference 1.2 for an overview of differences between the Standard/Alternate Forms and the Short Form.

Rapid Reference 1.2

Differences Between the CVLT-II Standard/Alternate Forms and the Short Form

Standard/alternate form	Short form
Administration	
16-word list from 4 categories	9-word list from 3 categories
5 Learning Trials	4 Learning Trials
Interference List and Recall	30-s distraction task
Short-Delay Free and Cued Recall	Short-Delay Free Recall
20-min delay	10-min delay
Long-Delay Free and Cued Recall	Long-Delay Free and Cued Recall
Long-Delay Yes/No Recognition	Long-Delay Yes/No Recognition
10-min Delay	5-min Delay
Forced-Choice Recognition	Forced-Choice Recognition
Scoring	
18 Hand-Scored Variables	15 Hand-Scored Variables
66 Normed Variables (Software)	51 Normed Variables (Software)
Multiple Raw Scores (Software)	

Scores derived on the CVLT-II assess attention, learning strategies, recall accuracy and consistency, proactive and retroactive interference, recall errors, recognition, and performance validity. Normative data are provided for 27 primary scores and 39 expanded scores in the scoring software. Eighteen of the primary variables can be hand scored. For the Short Form, 23 primary scores are provided along with 28 expanded scores in the scoring software. Fifteen of the primary variables can be hand scored. In addition, the scoring software provides raw data for numerous nonnormed variables in a research report.

A *T* score is derived for the learning trials (Trials 1–5 for Standard/Alternate Forms and Trials 1–4 for the Short Form) with a mean of 50 and a standard deviation of 10. The process scores provided in the CVLT-II provide detailed information about the learning and memory processes required to encode, recall, and recognize verbal information. For these scores, age- and gender-corrected *z* scores are provided with a mean of 0 and a standard deviation of 1. In addition, cumulative percentages are provided for some scores with highly skewed distributions. The normative scores derived in CVLT-II are listed in Rapid Reference 1.3 by condition.

Rapid Reference 1.3

Primary Scores Derived in CVLT-II, by Condition

Learning trials	Recall scores	Recognition scores
Trial 1 Free-Recall Correct[a] Trial 2 Free-Recall Correct[a] Trial 3 Free-Recall Correct[a] Trial 4 Free-Recall Correct[a] Trial 5 Free-Recall Correct[a,b] Trials 1–5 Free-Recall Correct (T score)[a] List B Free-Recall Correct[a,b] List B vs. Trial 1 (contrast score) Semantic Clustering (Chance-Adjusted) Semantic Clustering Bidirectional (Chance-Adjusted)	Short-Delay Free-Recall Correct[a] Short-Delay Cued Recall Correct[a,b] Short-Delay Free Recall vs Trial 5 (contrast score) Long-Delay Free-Recall Correct[a] Long-Delay Cued Recall Correct[a] Long-Delay Free Recall vs. Short-Delay Free Recall (contrast score) Free-Recall Intrusions[a] Cued-Recall Intrusions[a]	Long-Delay Yes/No Recognition Total Hits[a] Long-Delay Yes/No Recognition Total False Positives[a] Total Recognition Discriminability (*d'*) Total Recognition Discriminability vs. Long-Delay Free Recall (contrast score) Total Response Bias Long-Delay Forced-Choice Recognition Percent Total Accuracy[a]

(*continued*)

Learning trials	Recall scores	Recognition scores
Subjective Clustering (Chance-Adjusted)	Total Intrusions[a]	
Percent Recall from Primacy	Total Repetitions[a]	
Percent Recall from Middle	Total Recall Discriminability	
Percent Recall from Recency		
Total Learning Slope Trials 1–5		
Across-Trial Recall Consistency		

[a]Scores that are easily hand scored.
[b]Scores not on the Short Form.

Difference scores compare performance on one task to performance on another task. On CVLT-II, difference (or savings) scores are derived using the sex- and age-corrected *z*-scores. Change and difference scores should not replace the primary scores but are used to guide interpretation of differences observed across conditions. Detailed information on the interpretation of scores is provided in Chapter 4.

OVERVIEW AND ORGANIZATION OF THE CVLT3

The CVLT3 is the most recent revision to the CVLT. The revision was guided by the need for updated normative data, feedback from users and reviewers of the CVLT-II (both personal and published), and research utilizing the CVLT-II. In terms of content, the administration instructions and word lists were not modified but remain the same as in the CVLT-II. However, a few items on the forced-choice recognition trial were modified to increase sensitivity as a measure of performance validity. The alternate and short forms were also retained with similar modifications made to the forced-choice recognition trial.

The CVLT3 addressed many needs identified in the research literature and customer feedback. Revisions made in the CVLT3 included:

- updated norms for ages 16–90, using a nationally stratified sample matched to the U.S. population;
- application of a scaled score metric (mean = 10, SD = 3) over the *T* score and *z*-score metric to allow easier comparison to other measures;
- introduction of index scores (mean = 100, SD = 15) on the key memory and learning scores (Trials 1–5, total delayed recall, total recall);
- updated intrusion measures to reflect different types of memory errors;

- digital administration, recording, and scoring; and
- provision of demographic adjustments to age-adjusted scores for education and sex presented as *T* scores in the scoring software.

Detailed information on the modifications and improvements to the content, psychometric properties, and clinical utility of the CVLT3 are described in the *CVLT3 Manual.* An overview of the changes is provided in Rapid Reference 1.4.

Rapid Reference 1.4

Changes from CVLT-II to CVLT3

- New normative sample reflective of 2015 U.S. Census data
- Increased age range to 90
- Index scores on standard score metric (mean = 100, SD = 15)
- Primary scores on scaled score metric (mean = 10, SD = 3)
- Trials 1–5 Total score computed by summing scaled scores for Trials 1–5
- Norms provided are age corrected only
- Demographic adjustments to normative scores available for sex and education, presented as *T* scores
- Forced-choice recognition items modified to include only concrete distractors (abstract distractors were removed)
- New measures of across- and within-trial intrusions
- New measures of intrusion error types
- New yes/no recognition scores that describe the types of recognition errors

The CVLT3 introduced significant changes to the scoring of the CVLT-II. Although scores still measure the processes underlying attention, learning, and memory, the traditional *T* score and *z*-score metrics were changed to standard and scaled scores. This allows direct comparison to other measures commonly used in evaluations. Three index scores are derived by summing the scaled scores for the learning trials (Trials 1–5), for the delayed recall trials (free and cued recall), and for all recall trials (learning, interference, short delay, and long delay). For the primary process scores, age-corrected scaled scores were derived with a mean of 10 and a standard deviation of 3. In addition, cumulative percentages are provided for some scores that had highly skewed distributions. The normative scores derived in CVLT3 are listed in Rapid Reference 1.5 by condition.

Contrast scores are utilized for difference scores in CVLT3. Contrast scaled scores provide information about performance on one task adjusted for performance on another relevant task. Similar to the manner in which demographic adjustments are derived for normative scores, one score is adjusted to account for performance on a related but separate score. For example, the Long-Delay Free-Recall Correct vs. Short-Delay Free-Recall

Correct Contrast Scaled Score adjusts the long-delay score based on performance on short-delay recall. This accounts for differences in performance on delayed memory due to differences in immediate recall. The new score represents the examinee's performance on delayed memory in comparison to individuals of similar immediate memory ability. Because contrast scores utilize age-adjusted scaled scores, they are not further adjusted by age. Contrast scaled scores are provided at the scaled score level and are presented as scaled scores with a mean of 10 and a standard deviation of 3. Contrast scores are used to interpret scores in relation to similar ability peers; they do not replace subtest scaled scores and should not be substituted for primary scores in reports or to compute index scores. Detailed information on the interpretation of contrast scaled scores is provided in Chapter 4.

The CVLT3 introduces the use of demographic adjustments to norms. In addition to the age-adjusted normative scores, education, and sex adjustments are provided in the scoring software. The demographic adjustments are applied to the normative scores to produce *T* scores that account for education and sex differences.

Rapid Reference 1.5

Primary Scores Derived in CVLT3, by Condition

Learning trials	Recall scores	Recognition scores
Trial 1 Correct[a]	Short-Delay Free-Recall Correct[a]	Long-Delay Yes/No Recognition Total Hits[a]
Trial 2 Correct[a]	Short-Delay Cued-Recall Correct[a,b]	Long-Delay Yes/No Recognition Total False Positives[a]
Trial 3 Correct[a]	Short-Delay Free-Recall Correct vs. Trial 5 Correct (contrast score)	Recognition Discriminability (*d'*)
Trial 4 Correct[a]	Long-Delay Free-Recall Correct[a]	Recognition Discriminability Nonparametric
Trial 5 Correct[a,b]	Long-Delay Cued-Recall Correct[a]	Long-Delay Free-Recall vs. Recognition Discriminability (*d'*) (contrast score)
Trials 1–5 Correct (standard score)[a]	Delayed Recall Correct (standard score)	Long-Delay Forced-Choice Recognition Hits[a]
List B Correct[a,b]	Total Recall Correct (standard score)	Long-Delay Free-Recall Discriminability vs. Recognition Discriminability (*d'*) (contrast score)
List B Correct vs. Trial 1 Correct (contrast score)	Total Recall Responses (standard score)	

Learning trials	Recall scores	Recognition scores
	Long-Delay Free-Recall Correct vs. Trial 5 Correct (contrast score)	
	Long-Delay Free-Recall Correct vs. Short-Delay Free-Recall Correct (contrast score)	
	Total Intrusions[a]	

[a]Scores that are easily hand scored.
[b]Scores not on the Short Form.

THEORETICAL FOUNDATION

Learning and memory have long been of interest to psychologists, with William James first proposing the concepts of short-term and long-term memory in 1890. Short-term memory was described as finite with low durability unless it was encoded into long-term memory that was more lasting and of infinite capacity. Ebbinghaus' (1885) famous experiments on memory described the processes of learning and forgetting and introduced the concepts of the learning curve (rate at which information is acquired over repeated trials), serial position effects (how position within a series of words impacts recall), and the forgetting curve (rate at which one forgets information with most decay occurring within the first 20 min after learning). These early descriptions and investigations into memory laid the groundwork for modern memory assessment.

Despite Ebbinghaus' experiments on the processes of learning and memory, the assessment of these concepts has historically focused on the amount of information an individual could encode, consolidate, and recall. *Encoding* is the process of taking external information and transforming it into mental representations or memories. *Consolidation* is the process through which information in immediate memory is moved into long-term memory, and *retrieval* is the process of recalling information from storage. Focus on the amount of recalled information allows a global picture of memory ability, including the determination of the presence of memory disorders.

With the use of immediate and delayed recall, memory assessments often provide scores for short-term memory and long-term memory, again measuring the amount of information retained. *Short-term memory* is the momentary storage of information, lasting from a few seconds to a few minutes. Memories lasting from hours to years are considered stored in *long-term memory*. Long-term memory can be categorized as either *implicit* or *explicit* memory. *Implicit* or procedural memory involves involuntary learning from experiences without conscious awareness, such as learning to ride a bike or drive a car. *Explicit* or declarative memory involves the purposeful storage and retrieval of information. Explicit memory can further be divided into *semantic* (factual) and *episodic* (personal events and context) memory. When described in these terms, the CVLT versions are measures of explicit episodic verbal memory.

Processes of Memory

Edith Kaplan and colleagues introduced the process approach to cognitive assessment (Kaplan, 1988; Libon, Swenson, Ashendorf, Bauer, & Bowers, 2013) through their work at the Boston Veterans Administration Medical Center. This approach places importance on assessing not just *what* an individual is able to do but also *how* they do it. The approach utilizes overall test scores to assess the severity of impairment but emphasizes the analysis of the process through which test scores are achieved and errors made. Similar overall test scores can be obtained through very different processes. The development of the CVLT applied this process approach to learning and memory. Through studies involving individuals with brain injuries or disorders, strengths and weaknesses of memory processes were identified that differed across and within clinical populations. The instrument was refined to capture these processes and allow further investigation. So, although importance is placed on the primary measures of recall accuracy; critical attention is also given to the processes underlying performance.

Performance on memory specific measures is not only influenced by learning and memory processes but also by other cognitive functions. For example, attentional processes and learning strategies have an impact on the encoding and retrieval of verbal information. The interrelated nature of processes utilized across cognitive abilities requires that the assessment of memory include the assessment of these related processes. The CVLT versions measure the specific processes of learning and memory and processes related to the success and failure of encoding and retrieval of information. This allows examiners to examine differences in performance due to specific cognitive deficits. Figure 1.3 displays the processes measured directly within the CVLT editions.

The ability to encode information is highly dependent upon the ability to perceive and attend to information. Auditory attention is a key precursor for adequate memory retention. Individuals who have difficulty focusing on information long enough to encode it will not be able to retain that information over time. The first trial of the CVLT provides information on auditory attention span. It correlates highly with other measures of attention and is impaired in clinical groups with known attentional deficits, such as those with anxiety or mood disorders. Most individuals improve in overall recall across the learning trials, so comparison of performance across trials can assist in teasing out the influence of attention on memory problems.

Learning is the acquisition of new information. Historically it has been measured through overall recall across learning trials or by assessing the learning slope, the amount of information gained after the initial learning trial. These measures are included in the CVLT editions but the CVLT editions go further to evaluate learning strategies and characteristics and consistency of recall. Learning involves both passive and active strategies. Rote repetition is a passive strategy for recalling information that increases consolidation but does not involve increasing efficiency of encoding information. Repetition requires that information is repeated multiple times for encoding to occur. This type of learning

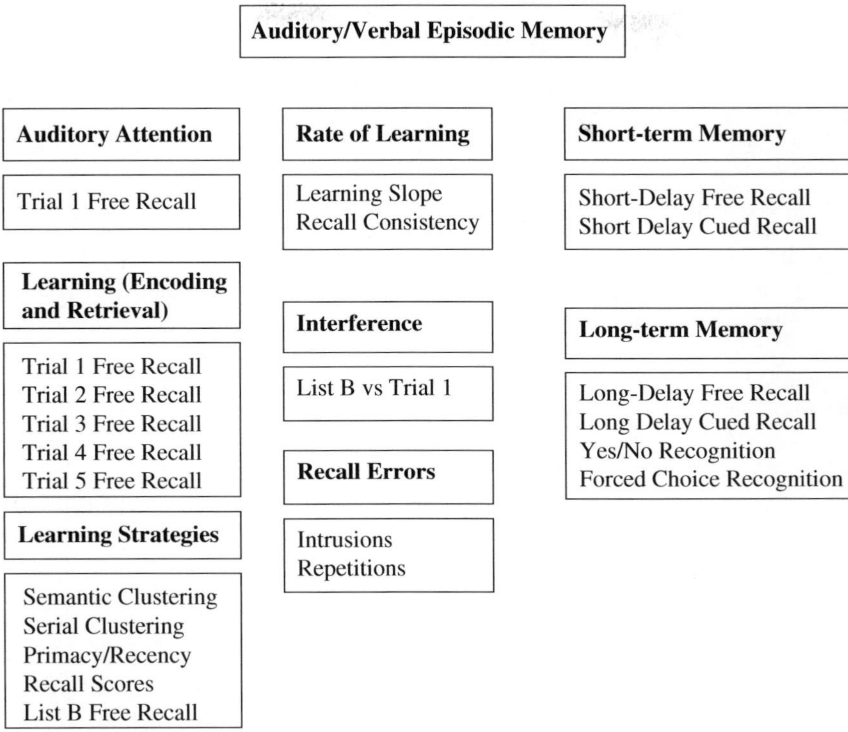

Figure 1.3. Memory processes measured in the CVLT.

strategy is represented in serial clustering or recalling words together that were close serially in the original list. Alternatively, active strategies of organizing information into meaningful groups aid the encoding and retrieval of information. The semantic grouping of words by an examinee represents utilization of this active learning strategy. Information on strategies used to encode information can aid in developing interventions for improving active learning.

In addition to evaluating learning strategies, data on the recall of words from different sections of the word list are provided. It is typical for individuals to recall more information from the beginning of a list (primacy effect) and from the end of a list (recency effect) than from the middle of a list. The primacy effect is generally attributed to greater rehearsal time for information whereas the recency effect is potentially related to the last words being held in recent or working memory. Examinees with encoding deficits often show higher recency effects than observed in the normative sample. Finally, consistency of recall provides information on the consistent application of recall strategies to retrieval of information. Individuals with executive functioning difficulties (e.g., poor planning, poor organization) often produce inconsistent profiles of responding. While this affects overall recall, executive functioning may be a key deficit in these cases.

The introduction of a second word list introduces active interference into the assessment of memory. Other measures utilize unrelated tasks to fill in between immediate and delayed recall but the CVLT actively introduces a second, similar list to explicitly assess interference. Two of the four semantic categories overlap across the two lists further eliciting interference effects. Comparison of performance on Trial 1 and the interference trial provides a measure of proactive interference, the decline in performance on learning material due to prior learning.

Whereas the level of recall on the immediate and delayed recall trials reflects overall retrieval, errors in recall provide insight into specific memory dysfunction and are invaluable in differential diagnoses. Repetitions or repeated responses are common in individuals with normal memory functioning when the repetition is used as self-cueing to promote further recall. However, repetitions can also be a sign of perseverative responding, the failure to inhibit previous responses, or poor self-monitoring. Intrusions, responses not from the current word list, are relatively uncommon in individuals without memory difficulties. Examination of the specific types of intrusions, which trials they occur on, their semantic relationships to the items in the word lists, and whether they are repeated across or within trials is critical to differentiating clinical groups. All clinical groups demonstrate deficits in memory recall; however, intrusions provide specific information about performance that aids in differentiating clinical groups.

Performance Validity

The assessment of performance validity has become standard practice in forensic and neuropsychological evaluations in both adult and pediatric populations (Brooks, Ploetz, & Kirkwood, 2016; Heilbronner et al., 2009; Holcomb, 2018; Martin, Schroeder, & Odland, 2015). The forced-choice task on the CVLT-II and CVLT3 was developed as an embedded measure of performance validity. In addition, Lichtenstein, Holcomb, and Erdodi (2018) presented data on a forced-choice measure developed for use with the CVLT-C. Several other scores across all three instruments have also demonstrated worth as indicators of performance validity, including recognition discriminability, Trials 1–5 Correct, Long-Delay Cued Recall, and Yes/No Recognition Hits (Bauer, Yantz, Ryan, Warden, & McCaffrey, 2005; Brooks & Ploetz, 2015; Shura, Miskey, Rowland, Yoash-Gantz, & Denning, 2016; Whiteside et al., 2015). It is important to note that low scores on these measures alone do not indicate invalid performance but suggest the possibility of symptom exaggeration or other factors that could influence performance.

RESEARCH FOUNDATION

Standardization and Psychometric Properties

Prior to evaluating the reliability data on the CVLT editions, it is important to note that estimates of reliability pose particular difficulties in measures of learning and recall. Measures of internal reliability do not accurately describe the reliability of memory measures due to item score interdependence. Recalling one word on a trial influences the recall of other words on a trial and also increases the likelihood of recalling the same word on further trials. For this reason, measures of test-retest reliability or alternate form reliability provide greater insight into the reliability of memory measures, although they are influenced by practice effects. Error measures or scores with limited variability also produce lower reliabilities due to skewed distributions. These limitations of traditional measures of reliability should be considered when interpreting the reliabilities described for the CVLT-C, CVLT-II, and CVLT3.

CVLT-C: The standardization sample for the CVLT-C consisted of 920 children selected to form a representative sample of the U.S. population, based on March 1988 U.S. Census data. It was stratified based on age, sex, race/ethnicity, education level, and geographic region. Twelve normative age bands were created, each included 1 year of age. Each age band for ages 5–12 included 80 children and bands for ages 13–16 included 70 children. Sex was roughly equal within each age group; all other demographic variables roughly matched the U.S. Census data.

Due to the interdependent nature of responses on word list recall, the CVLT-C utilized several measures of internal consistency. Internal consistency was evaluated using three approaches: comparing overall performance on odd and even numbered learning trials, across-semantic category consistency, and across-word consistency. The odd-even and across-word approaches yielded average correlations of 0.88 and 0.83, respectively, for Trials 1–5. The across-semantic category approach yielded an average correlation of 0.72. Detailed information on how these consistency estimates were defined and derived is provided in the *CVLT-C Manual*.

The test-retest sample consisted of 106 children tested between 10 and 42 days apart. Results are reported for three age groups: 8-, 12-, and 16-year-olds. Memory and learning measures are particularly susceptible to practice effects that lower test-retest correlations (Strauss, Sherman, & Spreen, 2006) due to repeated exposure of the stimuli to be recalled. Stability coefficients for 13 CVLT-C scores are listed in Rapid Reference 1.6. Test-retest coefficients ranged from 0.61 to 0.73 for the Trials 1–5 *T* score, from 0.26 to 0.77 for the recall *z*-scores, and from 0.17 to 0.90 for the error *z*-scores.

CVLT-II: The standardization sample for the CVLT-II consisted of 1,087 individuals selected to form a representative sample of the U.S. population, based on the March 1999 U.S. Census data. It was stratified based on age, sex, race/ethnicity, education level, and geographic region. Seven normative age bands were created: 16–19, 20–29, 30–44, 45–59, 60–69, 70–79, and 80–89. Each age band included between 107 and 200 individuals. Sex was evenly represented for ages 16–59; in ages 60–89 more females were included than males, reflecting the sex distribution in the population at the older ages.

Internal consistency was evaluated using the three approaches introduced in the CVLT-C: comparing overall performance on odd and even numbered learning trials, across-semantic category consistency, and across-trial word consistency. The odd-even and across-semantic category approaches yielded average correlations of 0.94 and 0.83, respectively, for Trials 1–5. The across-trial word consistency approach yielded an average correlation of 0.79. Estimates obtained in a clinical sample of 124 neuropsychiatric patients produced similar reliability coefficients. Detailed information on how these consistency estimates were defined and derived is provided in the *CVLT-II Manual*.

Rapid Reference 1.6

Stability Coefficients for 13 CVLT-C Scores, by Age

Score	Age 8 average test-retest r_{12}	Age 12 average test-retest r_{12}	Age 16 average test-retest r_{12}
List A Trials 1–5 Total	0.73	0.73	0.61
List B Free Recall Total	0.59	0.26	0.66
Short-Delay Free Recall	0.40	0.77	0.48
Short-Delay Cued Recall	0.75	0.49	0.59
Long-Delay Free Recall	0.59	0.62	0.60
Long-Delay Cued Recall	0.69	0.69	0.59
Semantic Cluster Ratio	0.56	0.58	0.53
Perseverations	0.90	0.32	0.31
Free-Recall Intrusions	0.74	0.56	0.85
Cued-Recall Intrusions	0.59	0.17	0.74
Recognition Hits	0.38	0.24	0.80
Discriminability	0.55	0.37	0.78
False Positives	0.62	0.35	0.78

Standardization data from the *California Verbal Learning Test, Children's Version (CVLT-C)*.

The test-retest sample consisted of 78 individuals tested between 9 and 49 days apart. Stability coefficients for 18 CVLT-II scores are listed in Rapid Reference 1.7. Test-retest coefficients were 0.82 for the Trials 1–5 *T* score, ranged from 0.57 to 0.88 for the recall *z*-scores, and from 0.27 to 0.86 for the error *z*-scores.

Due to the addition of the Alternate Form, alternate form reliability was also provided. The Alternate Form sample consisted of 288 nonclinical adults tested between 0 and 77 days apart. The administrations were counterbalanced, with 155 receiving the Standard Form first followed by the Alternate Form and 133 receiving the Alternate Form first followed by the Standard Form. Correlation coefficients for the 18 scores that can be hand scored are listed in Rapid Reference 1.8. Correlation coefficients were 0.79 for the Trials 1–5 *T* score, ranged from 0.51 to 0.76 for the recall *z* scores, and ranged from 0.27 to 0.76 for the error *z* scores.

Rapid Reference 1.7

Stability Coefficients for CVLT-II Scores, by Age

Score	Average test-retest r_{12}
Trials 1–5 Correct (*T* score)	0.82
Trial 1 Correct	0.57
Trial 2 Correct	0.60
Trial 3 Correct	0.58
Trial 4 Correct	0.82
Trial 5 Correct	0.76
Trial B Correct	0.61
Short-Delay Free-Recall Correct	0.81
Long-Delay Free-Recall Correct	0.88
Semantic Clustering (Chance-Adjusted) Trials 1–5	0.74
Total Learning Slope, Trials 1–5	0.27
Total Intrusions	0.63
Total Repetitions	0.30
Long-Delay Yes/No Recognition Hits	0.79
Long-Delay Yes/No Recognition False Positives	0.72
Total Recognition Discrimination	0.86
Total Response Bias	0.57

Standardization data from the *California Verbal Learning Test, Second Edition Adult Version (CVLT-II)*.

CVLT3: The standardization sample for the CVLT3 consisted of 700 individuals selected to form a representative sample of the U.S. population, based on 2015 U.S. Census data. It was stratified based on age, sex, race/ethnicity, education level, and geographic region. Seven normative age bands were created: 16–19, 20–29, 30–44, 45–59, 60–69, 70–79, and 80–90. Each age band included 100 individuals. Sex was evenly represented for ages 16–59 and in proportion to the U.S. Census in ages 60–90.

Internal consistency was evaluated using alternate form reliability. The Alternate Form sample consisted of 213 nonclinical adults administered the Standard and Alternate Forms

Rapid Reference 1.8

Alternate Form Reliability for the CVLT-II

Score	Average test-retest r_{12}
Trials 1–5 Correct (*T* score)	0.79
Trial 1 Correct	0.52
Trial 2 Correct	0.61
Trial 3 Correct	0.71
Trial 4 Correct	0.70
Trial 5 Correct	0.71
Trial B Correct	0.51
Short-Delay Free-Recall Correct	0.73
Long-Delay Free-Recall Correct	0.76
Semantic Clustering (Chance-Adjusted) Trials 1–5	0.61
Semantic Clustering (Chance-Adjusted) Trials 1–5	0.35
Total Learning Slope, Trials 1–5	0.38
Total Intrusions	0.55
Total Repetitions	0.46
Long-Delay Yes/No Recognition Hits	0.64
Long-Delay Yes/No Recognition False Positives	0.76
Total Recognition Discrimination	0.72
Total Response Bias	0.55
Forced-Choice Recognition Percent Total Accuracy	0.68

of the CVLT3 between 10 and 51 days apart. The administrations were counterbalanced, with 107 receiving the Standard Form first followed by the Alternate Form and 106 receiving the Alternate Form first followed by the Standard Form. Correlation coefficients are reported in the *CVLT3 Manual* for all normed scores for two age groups: 16–44 and 45–90. Alternate form correlations for the 18 core and index scores are listed in Rapid Reference 1.9. Correlation coefficients ranged from 0.79 to 0.83 for the index scores, from 0.50 to 0.71 for the recall scaled scores, from 0.49 to 0.67 for the recognition scaled scores, and from 0.15 to 0.66 for the error and process scaled scores.

Rapid Reference 1.9

Alternate Form Reliability for the CVLT3 Core and Index Scores

Score	Ages 16–44 average test-retest r_{12}	Ages 45–90 average test-retest r_{12}
Trials 1–5 Correct (Standard score)	0.75	0.80
Trial 1 Correct	0.51	0.56
Trial 2 Correct	0.53	0.59
Trial 3 Correct	0.70	0.63
Trial 4 Correct	0.58	0.67
Trial 5 Correct	0.50	0.71
List B Correct	0.57	0.53
Short-Delay Free-Recall Correct	0.71	0.71
Short-Delay Cued-Recall Correct	0.56	0.69
Long-Delay Free-Recall Correct	0.61	0.71
Long-Delay Cued-Recall Correct	0.60	0.65
Delayed Recall Correct (Standard Score)	0.77	0.80
Total Recall Correct (Standard Score)	0.79	0.83
Total Intrusions	0.25	0.57
Yes/No Recognition Hits	0.49	0.62
Yes/No Recognition False Positives	0.57	0.55
Recognition Discrimination	0.67	0.54
Recognition Discrimination Nonparametric	0.65	0.58

Effect sizes ranged from −0.09 to 0.06 across the index scores, from −0.11 to 0.11 across the recall scaled scores, from −0.15 to 0.06 across the recognition scaled scores, and from −0.18 to 0.29 across the error and process scaled scores, indicating small changes in performance across forms. Therefore, it is unlikely that

CAUTION 1.1

Memory and learning measures are particularly susceptible to practice effects. Practice effects can be observed for more than 6 months.

performance will vary across the two forms greatly due to experience with the test. It is important to note that when the same form is administered, memory tests show practice effects (i.e., performance improvement related to prior experience with taking a test) for a long time after administration, with patients recalling information for months to years after administration (Goldberg, Harvey, Wesnes, Snyder, & Schneider, 2015).

COMPREHENSIVE REFERENCES ON TEST

The most detailed and comprehensive information for each edition of the CVLT can be found in the corresponding test manual: *CVLT-C Manual, CVLT-II Manual,* and *CVLT3 Manual.* Each manual provides an overview of the test, descriptions of each condition and score, and detailed information on administration and scoring, calculating the raw scores, and deriving normative scores. Information on the theoretical underpinnings, development and standardization, reliability, validity, and interpretation are also provided. In addition, the *CVLT3 manual* provides an overview of the use of demographic adjustments to the CVLT3 norms.

Editions of the CVLT have been used in multiple research studies incorporated into thousands of published articles. The CVLT-C has been used to assess memory functioning in typically developing children, children with acquired disorders, such as brain tumors and injuries, and children with neurological disorders, such as epilepsy. The CVLT-II has been used to examine memory functioning in typically developing and aging adults, individuals with degenerative diseases, such as mild cognitive impairment and dementia, individuals with acquired injuries, such as stroke or traumatic brain injury, individuals with psychiatric disorders, such as schizophrenia, and other populations with suspected or known memory disorders. It is expected that more research on the CVLT3 will become available as the revision is more widely used. Rapid Reference 1.10 provides basic reference and publication information for the CVLT-C, CVLT-II, and CVLT3.

Rapid Reference 1.10

Publication Data for CVLT-C

Authors: Dean C. Delis, Joel H. Kramer, Edith Kaplan, and Beth A. Ober
Publication Date: 1994
What test measures: Verbal and Auditory Learning and Memory
Age Range: 5–16
Administration Time: 30 min administration plus a 20-min delay
Qualification of Examiners: Graduate- or professional-level training in psychological assessment
Publisher: NCS Pearson, Inc.
5601 Green Valley Drive
Bloomington, MN 55437
Order Phone Number: 1-800-627-7271
www.PearsonClinical.com
Price: Complete Kit: (as of March 2019) $235.75 (paper kit); 107.00 (scoring software)

Publication Data for CVLT-II

Authors: Dean C. Delis, Joel H. Kramer, Edith Kaplan, and Beth A. Ober
Publication Date: 2000
What test measures: Verbal and Auditory Learning and Memory
Age Range: 16–89
Administration Time:
Standard and Alternate Forms: 30 min administration plus 20-min delay (optional 10-min delay before optional 5-min forced-choice recognition condition)
Short Form: 20 min administration plus 10-min delay (optional 5-min delay before optional 5-min forced-choice recognition condition)
Qualification of Examiners: Graduate- or professional-level training in psychological assessment
Publisher: NCS Pearson, Inc.
5601 Green Valley Drive
Bloomington, MN 55437
Order Phone Number: 1-800-627-7271
www.PearsonClinical.com
Price: Complete Kit: (as of March 2019) $136.50 (manual); 105.00 (25 Standard/Alternate Record Forms); 84.00 (25 Short Record Forms); Digital Scoring priced by usage and subscription

Publication Data for CVLT3

Authors: Dean C. Delis, Joel H. Kramer, Edith Kaplan, and Beth A. Ober
Publication Date: 2017
What test measures: Verbal and Auditory Learning and Memory
Age Range: 5–16
Administration Time:
Standard and Alternate Forms: 30-min administration plus 20-min delay (optional 10-min delay before optional 5-min forced-choice recognition condition)
Short Form: 20-min administration plus 10-min delay (optional 5-min delay before optional 5-min forced-choice recognition condition)
Qualification of Examiners: Graduate- or professional-level training in psychological assessment
Publisher: NCS Pearson, Inc.
5601 Green Valley Drive
Bloomington, MN 55437
Order Phone Number: 1-800-627-7271
www.PearsonClinical.com
Price: Complete Kit: (as of March 2019) $409.00 (paper kit); 430.00 (paper kit plus 1-year online scoring subscription)

A NOTE ON CVLT NOMENCLATURE

There is a great deal of overlap in the structure, administration, scoring, and interpretation of the CVLT versions. For ease of communication, CVLT is used throughout this guide to refer to all three versions presented. This allows for quick communication of information without listing each individual measure. In instances where CVLT refers to the original publication, this is indicated within the text. Moreover, when information is specific to one version of the CVLT, this is clearly indicated.

TEST YOURSELF

1. **Memory measures like the CVLT help differentiate normal, age-related decline from deficits related to disruption or impairment of memory processes.**
   True or False
2. **The California Verbal Learning Test was developed using in the process approach. This means that although ___________ are important in determining severity of a memory impairment or what a person can do, ___________ provide key information on how a person achieves those scores.**
   (a) overall recall scores, process scores
   (b) process scores, behavioral characteristics
   (c) error scores, immediate and delayed recall scores
   (d) error scores, process scores
3. **The CVLT-C was designed specifically for children ages 5–16. What is the main difference between the structure of the CVLT-C and the CVLT-II?**
   (a) The word lists are divided into semantic categories on CVLT-II.
   (b) The word lists are shorter on CVLT-C and involve categories for children.
   (c) CVLT-C reflects developmental processes specific to children.
   (d) The structure of the CVLT-C and CVLT-II are the same
4. **The Forced-Choice Recognition condition was added after the original CVLT. What was this condition specifically designed to measure?**
   (a) Recall errors
   (b) Recognition memory
   (c) Learning characteristics
   (d) Performance validity
5. **Semantic clustering, serial clustering, and serial position effects are all:**
   (a) learning strategies and characteristics
   (b) ways to enhance recall of information
   (c) measures of immediate and delayed memory
   (d) measures of recognition memory
6. **Why is reliability in memory assessments difficult to assess?**
   (a) Items are not scored individually
   (b) Trials are not scored individually
   (c) Items are not independent
   (d) Scores on memory measures are skewed

7. **All scores on CVLT-C, CVLT-II, and CVLT3 can be hand scored.**
   True or False
8. **Which of the following is a major change introduced in the CVLT3?**
   (a) new word lists were created for CVLT3
   (b) an alternate form and a short form were introduced
   (c) the age range was extended down to 5
   (d) normative scores are not corrected for gender only
9. **Memory processes are influenced by cognitive abilities other than specific encoding, storage, and retrieval functions.**
   True or False
10. **Practice effects on memory tests:**
    (a) are negligible.
    (b) can be observed for months or years.
    (c) are not relevant in clinical populations.
    (d) are short lived, similar to other cognitive measures.

Answers: 1. True, 2. a, 3. b, 4. d, 5. a, 6. c, 7. False, 8. d, 9. True, 10. b

Two

HOW TO ADMINISTER THE CVLT-C, CVLT-II, AND CVLT3

When administered appropriately, the California Verbal Learning Test (CVLT) provides detailed information on the processes involved in learning and memory. Adhering to standardized testing procedures is key to ensuring valid, usable results, ensures consistent administration, decreases measurement error, and increases the reliability of results obtained across examiners. Pay close attention to the directions of each trial to ensure the appropriate use of prompting throughout administration. Modifications to the standardized administration, recording, and scoring instructions should always be noted in reports and considered when interpreting normative data. Significant deviations may not result in valid application of the norms.

There is a great degree of overlap between the administration of the child and adult versions of the CVLT; however, there are administrative differences that need to be followed. Detailed instructions on arranging the testing environment, building rapport during administration, adhering to standard administration guidelines, and recording responses are provided in the *CVLT-C, CVLT-II,* and *CVLT3 Manuals*. Before using any of the CVLT editions, familiarize yourself with the administration guidelines and instructions. This chapter provides an overview of administration guidelines for the CVLT and describes differences between the editions. Familiarizing yourself with the information in this chapter and the detailed directions in the manuals, along with administering a practice case, will help you prepare for using the CVLT with patient populations.

APPROPRIATE TESTING CONDITIONS

Testing Environment

The environment in which a test is administered can have an impact on an examinee's performance. The ideal testing environment for the CVLT is a quiet, well-lit, comfortably ventilated and heated/cooled room free from distractions. The examinee should sit with his or her back to any large visual distractions, such as windows or computer monitors. Distractions can interrupt the learning and recall process so minimize interruptions during testing. For example, when testing in a school, attempt to schedule the test session around class transition times to avoid bells or loud hallway noise. In addition, no one other than you and the examinee should be in the room during testing. This reduces the social distraction of another individual, eliminates the possibility of explicit or inadvertent cueing by the third person, and reduces deferential or dependent behavior by the examinee. However, in some cases, this is not feasible due to the specific needs of an examinee. For example, when an examinee requires a caregiver to remain for personal care. In these cases, speak to the caregiver prior to the test session to prepare them for the test session. Any third person who will be present during administration should be instructed on appropriate behavior during the test session, including behaviors that are not allowed during the test session, such as responding to items or aiding the examinee in responding to items. You may also want to address limitations on interacting with the examinee to increase the likelihood that answers will not be discussed or cues given (e.g., pointing to something related to a word on the list). It may be helpful to explain the purpose of the assessment and describe the standard administration procedures to ensure that the examinee's results are valid and interpretable. If a caregiver expresses concern about knowing if it is appropriate to interact with or assist the examinee, you may suggest that you will ask them for assistance when it is needed or if preferred, that they ask before assisting during the testing session. Establishing expectations before the testing session will help avoid confusion during the session. Every effort should be made to ensure the examinee's performance is not negatively affected by the testing environment. Never make assumptions about the environment on behalf of the examinee—for example, the room temperature may be comfortable for you but could be too hot or too cool for the examinee.

Plan an appropriate length of time for testing or divide testing into multiple sessions. Although the CVLT needs to be administered within a single session, multiple sessions may be needed to complete a longer battery of tests that includes the CVLT. Regardless, administer all desired trials and conditions of CVLT in the same session. During testing, the examinee should sit across from you to allow you to fully observe the examinee throughout testing. This also places the directions or items on the record form or Q-interactive screen out of view of the examinee. All directions and word lists are included on the record form or screen. Throughout testing, the record form or screen should be placed so that the instructions are not visible to the examinee. The use of a clipboard when using the record form provides a hard surface on which to record responses without exposing the stimuli. You will also need access to a clock or watch in order to ensure the appropriate delay time is given between the learning and short-delay trials and the long-delay trials. Keep an eye out for signs of discomfort in the examinee, such as increased shifting in the chair or fidgeting, and take a break or adjust the room accordingly. Be sure any break does not interrupt the learning trials; the best time for a break in CVLT is during the delay times.

Be mindful that examinees may use a wide range of methods to remember the word list. For example, they may use rote rehearsal in their mind or they may employ mental mnemonic techniques. Observable signs of strategies for remembering information are good to observe and note during testing. Close attention to the examinee can also allow you to catch examinees engaging in inappropriate behaviors. An examinee may attempt to capture information by writing words on their hand or on the table or even entering words into their phone. Although this may be an appropriate strategy for recalling information outside of the test session, it would invalidate the results of the CVLT. It is critical to pay attention to the examinee while administering the CVLT and other cognitive tests to ensure examinees engage in appropriate behavior throughout the test session.

Testing Materials

The CVLT does not require any materials to complete administration other than the appropriate record form. Detailed scoring information is provided in the relevant test manual for obtaining scores upon completion of the test session; however, the manual is not required for administration. Scores are automatically provided following administration of CVLT on Q-interactive once each response is classified as correct, incorrect, intrusion, or repetition. Chapter 3 provides detailed information on how to classify responses. Scores can also be obtained through the CVLT-C and CVLT-II scoring software or through the Q-global platform for CVLT3. It is important to note that the software for CVLT-C and CVLT-II has not been updated since the original publication of these products and may not be compatible with current operating systems.

CAUTION 2.1

Materials Required for Administering the CVLT-C, CVLT-II, and CVLT3

- Paper
  - record form
  - watch or clock
  - pencil or pen for examiner
  - clipboard
- Digital
  - iPad with Q-interactive Assess app (practitioner)
  - stylus

TRIAL ADMINISTRATION SEQUENCE

When administering any form on any of the CVLT editions, the trials should be presented in the order presented in the record form. The Long-Delay Forced-Choice Recognition task is the only optional task on the CVLT and is the last task administered. If you choose not to administer Forced-Choice Recognition, simply stop administration after Long-Delay Yes/No Recognition. Note that Forced-Choice Recognition is not included in the CVLT-C; therefore, all tasks must be administered on the CVLT-C.

CAUTION 2.2

Appropriate Delay Tasks

Visual Memory Tasks (Rey-Osterrieth Complex Figure, Visual Reproduction)

Visual Fluid Reasoning Tasks (Matrix Reasoning)

Visual Processing Tasks (Block Design)

Visual Processing Speed Tasks (Coding, Symbol Span)

Visual Executive Functioning Tasks (Trail Making, Wisconsin Card Sort)

CAUTION 2.3

Do not administer the CVLT after another word list task if administered within a battery of tests.

For example:

Verbal Paired Associates in WMS-IV

Verbal Learning in Wide Range Assessment of Memory and Learning, Second Edition (Sheslow & Adams, 2003)

Rey Auditory Verbal Learning Test (Schmidt, 1996)

Hopkins Verbal Learning Test—Revised (Benedict, Schretlen, Groninger, & Brandt, 1998)

NEPSY Word Learning (Korkman, Kirk, & Kemp, 2007)

Children's Memory Scale Word List (Cohen, 1997)

Due to the delay required between short-delay and long-delay trials, it is important to plan ahead and have appropriate tasks to complete during this delay time. The tasks should fill between 15 and 25 min. Appropriate nonverbal measures to administer during this delay include visual working memory measures (e.g., Wechsler Memory Scale—Fourth Edition Symbol Span (WMS-IV; Wechsler, 2009), Wechsler Intelligence Scale for Children—Fifth Edition Picture Span (WISC-V; Wechsler, 2015)), visual memory measures (e.g., Rey-Osterrieth Complex Figure (Osterreith, 1944; Rey, 1941)), nonverbal processing speed measures (e.g., WISC-V Coding), or other nonverbal measures (e.g., Delis-Kaplan Executive Function System Trail Making; Delis, Kaplan, & Krammer, 2001). The key element of these tasks is that they are nonverbal so that they don't tax or interfere with the verbal encoding and recall of the CVLT word list. The Short Form of the CVLT-II and Brief Form of the CVLT3 also require additional tasks to be administered; however, the delay time is shorter, approximately 10 min, so shorter tasks should be used.

ADMINISTERING CVLT-II OR CVLT3 SHORT FORM

Although some examinees may become frustrated or refuse to complete all trials; in order to obtain *all* the available standard, scaled, and process scores, all tasks within the CVLT need to be administered. If an examinee does not complete the full CVLT, certain scores may still be obtained based on how many trials were completed; however, the comprehensive evaluation of an individual's learning and memory processes is significantly limited in such situations. The CVLT is frequently used within a larger assessment battery designed by the examiner to address learning and memory ability within the broader context of other cognitive skills. CVLT's relatively short administration time in relation to other memory measures makes it a useful tool within broader assessments. However, there are instances where even the 40 min (15 min of administration time and 25 min of delay) required for CVLT standard and alternate forms may be too long and the short form of the CVLT-II or brief form of the CVLT3 is desired.

When choosing to administer the shorter forms, it is important to ensure you obtain the information you need to answer the referral question. The short forms do not have the same number of trials or include an interference trial as the standard and alternate forms. Therefore, fewer scores are available when using these forms. If the referral question relates to recall of information following distraction, the standard or alternate forms may be more appropriate. Alternately, if the referral is to screen for memory impairment or involves an individual whose tolerance for testing may be limited due to medical reasons, the shorter forms may be more appropriate.

ADMINISTERING CVLT VIA TELEPRACTICE

Psychological assessment is slowly adapting to new approaches to addressing patient needs. Telepractice or remote testing is becoming increasingly common to address a lack of available practitioners, cost for services, and transportation requirements for patients. The Bureau of Veterans Affairs, rural school districts, and other agencies are implementing telepractice within their systems (see Yoder and Turner [2014] for an overview of the use of telemedicine with veterans). Typically, the examinee goes to a nearby medical or office location and initial setup is completed by staff in that location. The assessment practitioner is then linked to the patient via virtual communication tools that include a video system. In some locations, a technician will remain in the room with the examinee to ensure continued connectivity or to present physical materials to the examinee. The exact logistics of each telepractice vary and if you chose to utilize this approach, you must be familiar with the resources and options available to you.

The CVLT is ideal, in many ways, for telepractice administration. If the virtual connection is uninterrupted and the audio to both you and the examinee and is clear, no additional physical materials are required for administration. Ensure the connection is clear by speaking with the examinee prior to beginning testing and watching for any signs of poor audibility, such as leaning toward the camera, trying to turn up the volume, or asking you to repeat what you have said. Do not begin administration of CVLT until you are sure the connection is clear and the volume is comfortable for the examinee. Throughout testing, watch for signs that the examinee does not understand or is uncomfortable so that you can address these as needed. Also, if a technician or staff member does not remain in the room, ensure you can observe the examinee completely. Examinees may engage in behaviors, such as writing down the words, playing on their phone, or answering e-mails, when alone in a room that are relatively rare when in a room with another person during testing. Also ensure you have a way to reach staff in the remote site if a medical need arises during testing.

Less frequently, telepractice may involve testing an examinee in his or her home. Although all of the same cautions should be observed as when an examinee is tested in an office, there are additional considerations. Before beginning testing, convey to the examinee the need to eliminate interruptions. Schedule testing when children, pets, or visitors are not expected and ask him or her to connect to the test session in a quiet location. Be aware of any environmental issues that may influence appropriate engagement in and completion of testing. Special caution should be taken with testing children in this manner to ensure parents or other adults are not assisting the child with responses.

No studies have been conducted with the CVLT to ensure the applicability of the norms when administered outside of the traditional in-person office setting.

However, given the lack of physical materials required for the examinee and due diligence by you to ensure appropriate engagement and participation, it is likely that results obtained via telepractice would be valid and interpretable.

DEVELOPING RAPPORT WITH EXAMINEES

Establishing Rapport

Rapport with an examinee is required to ensure appropriate interest, motivation, and participation in testing. Standardized tests require the ability to establish rapport with examinees. Memory testing may be especially difficult for many examinees as the long-term impacts of memory impairments may be aversive, particularly for older adults who are concerned about progressive memory decline. For many examinees, results of the assessment are tied to access to programs, medications, interventions, and other benefits or are part of receiving a diagnosis that may affect their lives. Establishing and maintaining rapport with the examinee is critical in these situations to reduce anxiety and stress during testing and elicit optimal performance.

Building rapport is unique for each examinee. The purpose of the testing, the testing environment, potential benefits and impacts of test results, familiarity with the examiner or testing, intrinsic motivation, and other related factors will influence the relationship between the examinee and examiner. Your experience and your knowledge of the examinee will help guide your approach to engaging the examinee and building rapport. Examinees differ in the need for conversation and relationship building but conversing with the examinee prior to the beginning of the session will demonstrate interest in the examinee and help build rapport. Clearly explain the purpose of the evaluation, including an overview of what types of tasks will be presented, and address any questions and concerns raised by the examinee or other individuals present. Be prepared to address the potential use of results, including whether results will be shared with a third party, such as in a forensic evaluation. Frequently, a parent, friend, or care provider may accompany the examinee during this initial meeting and discussion. This allows support for the examinee, provides a secondary source of information, and allows you to address any questions the examinee may be unable to answer. When an examinee is young, has communication difficulties, is uncooperative or resistant to being evaluated, or is easily overwhelmed or confused, the additional support provided by the third person can assist in transitioning into the testing session. Building rapport will vary across examinees in both the time required and style but is a vital part of preparing yourself and the examinee for the test session.

Memory testing frequently elicits emotional concerns from examinees; plan to address concerns about performance directly with the examinee. You can provide a basic overview of the testing session, including information on the length of the testing session, a description of the planned tasks and activities, and how performance will be evaluated and reported. For example, older adults are often comforted to know that performance on memory measures are compared to similar age peers, not to younger adults. Detailed information on the content is not recommended nor is a lengthy description of the session; however, preparing the examinee for sustained effort might help elicit the examinee's best effort during testing. Finally, it is important to address any concerns the examinee may have regarding the potential use of results (e.g., loss of independence, financial or medical decision making, legal proceedings).

Forensic evaluations and other evaluations in which a third party will receive results require special attention. It is important to address the ownership and use of results and to assure the examinee that an accurate assessment of his or her strengths and weaknesses will best be achieved with good cooperation and effort. Any legal restrictions on sharing of information or implications of inadequate participation in testing should be addressed directly. Most examinees referred for testing are willing to participate and give good effort; however, there are circumstances in which an examinee may not demonstrate consistent effort or may refuse to complete testing. In these cases, stopping and rescheduling the test session may be the best approach if cooperation is more likely at a later time. Measures of performance validity (e.g., Advanced Clinical Solutions for WAIS-IV [Wechsler Adult Intelligence Scale] and WMS-IV [Wechsler Memory Scale]; Pearson, 2009, Test of Memory and Malingering, Tombaugh, 1996) should also be a standard part of test administration. The Association for Scientific Advancement in Psychological Injury and Law (Bush, Heilbronner, & Ruff, 2014) developed guidelines for the appropriate and ethical use of performance validity measures, including inclusion in informed consent prior to testing.

Maintaining Rapport

Remember that rapport can be easily lost and may need to be reestablished throughout the assessment. Maintaining rapport requires your full attention throughout the test session. Learn and internalize the administration and recording of the CVLT prior to administration so that you can focus your attention on the examinee. During administration, encourage continued effort by praising the examinee's effort and persistence (e.g., "You're working hard"). Never indicate that a specific response was correct or incorrect or provide additional presentation of the word list beyond the learning trials. Statements of support and reassurance should be tied to the examinee's needs and provide encouragement rather than induce unease. Be aware of how the examinee responds to feedback and adjust as needed.

TESTING INDIVIDUALS WITH SPECIAL NEEDS

Given the verbal requirements of the CVLT, hearing impairments will likely affect performance on the CVLT. Because auditory deficits increase with age, older adults may be particularly vulnerable to performance declines on CVLT due to hearing difficulty. Armstrong et al. (2018) found declines in CVLT performance on learning, short-delay, and long-delay recall trials across two testing sessions conducted several years apart; these declines were not related to memory ability at initial assessment but were related to hearing impairment. It is essential to know of any hearing impairments an examinee has prior to testing with the CVLT so that you can ensure appropriate accommodations are in place prior to testing (e.g., amplification devices).

Language and cultural influences, such as fluency in English, are also important to ascertain prior to testing to ensure that the instruments selected for the test session are appropriate for the specific examinee being assessed. For some examinees, such as individuals with expressive language difficulties, significant hearing impairments, or who are non-English speakers, the CVLT may not be an appropriate measure.

For most examinees, standard administration directions can be used to administer the CVLT. Standard administration should be followed when possible as this provides the greatest opportunity for obtaining valid test results. Providing modifications or accommodations limits the use of standard scores and should be used only when necessary, such as when the nature of the client's impairment may mask the examinee's true ability when CVLT is administered under standard conditions. If an examinee's differences influence performance on the CVLT or modifications are made to the standard administration procedures to accommodate for a difference, it is imperative to note this in the report and consider this during the interpretation of results. Attributing low performance to memory impairment alone when other factors influenced performance may result in harm to an examinee, including possible misdiagnosis, inappropriate treatment, loss of access to services, loss of independence, or other adverse outcomes.

When modifications are necessary to ensure meaningful data and these modifications are appropriately documented and considered, meaningful information may still be obtained with the CVLT. Small changes to standard procedures may not have an impact on the validity of results while providing a clear picture of an examinee's verbal memory abilities. However, there are limited data to support modifications so your clinical experience and judgment will be needed to determine whether a modification limits the applicability of normative data. The degree of modification to the administration or response requirements can help guide these decisions. For example, increased volume and articulation of the words during the presentation of the word list may assist examinees with hearing difficulties and allow valid normative comparisons. However, presenting the words in written format so that an examinee may read the words may allow examinees with profound hearing deficits to complete the CVLT but this modification significantly changes the test. In this case, the modifications likely influenced performance enough for the use of normed scores to be questionable. In some cases, questionable results are better than no results; use you clinical judgment to determine whether results obtained in this manner are helpful for a particular examinee. Rapid Reference 2.1 provides some suggestions on modifying the CVLT to accommodate individuals with special needs. It is important to note any accommodations from the standard administration in your final report and on the record form. For more information on modifying instruments for examinees with special needs, see Mitrushina, Boone, Razani, and D'Elia (2005); Salvia, Ysseldyke, and Bolt (2013); Strauss, Sherman, and Spreen (2006); and/or Vanderploeg (2000).

Rapid Reference 2.1

Modifications to the CVLT Administration to Accommodate an Examinee's Special Needs

Hearing Difficulties

Within standard administration: Ensure the testing environment is quiet and free from outside noise. Sit in close proximity to the examinee and sit on the side with better hearing, if applicable. Although speaking in a louder tone or with enhanced articulation may help, it can also distort speech so assess whether speaking more loudly helps before doing so throughout the assessment. You may repeat directions but do not repeat items. Have the examinee repeat instructions back to you to ensure clear communication. When facing the examinee, ensure the examinee can clearly see your face as this may help decode speech. Affirming a repeated response during reading of the word lists by nodding if the examinee repeats it back as a question.

Beyond standard administration: Provide written instructions to help communicate instructions. Provide written stimuli for the word lists. Verifying accurate hearing by having the examinee repeat words immediately after presentation or the word list.

Visual Difficulties

Within standard administration: No visual abilities are required for performance on CVLT.

Motor Difficulties

Within standard administration: No motor abilities are required for performance on CVLT.

Communication Difficulties

Beyond standard administration: For recognition items, allow pointing to responses instead of verbal responses when appropriate.

Allow written responses to verbal subtests. Rephrase instructions to increase comprehension. Redirect if responses do not make sense.

Non-English Speakers

Beyond standard administration: Use an interpreter during testing. Administer the test in the language spoken by the examinee. Use a translated version of the test.

CVLT was designed for use with fluent English speakers. Although the use of the CVLT with non-native speakers may allow for the application of normative data, its use with non-fluent or non-English speakers deviates significantly from standard administration. Ideally, validated translations of CVLT would be available in every language needed in clinical settings; in reality, CVLT is not officially translated into any languages although several translated versions have been used in research (e.g., Costers et al., 2017; Poreh, Avital, Dines, & Levin, 2015). The use of an interpreter, using a translated or adapted research version, or administering the test bilingually or in the examinee's language, may be utilized with the CVLT, but each of these approaches limits the validity of using the normative data and may violate copyright. Because word difficulty and frequency of use vary across languages, a direct translation will not account for these differences. Any application of normative data obtained in this manner must be noted in your report and likely does not reflect the examinee's true verbal memory processes and abilities.

Testing Older Adults

Older adults frequently present with memory concerns and assessing memory processes is a key part of every evaluation with older adults, even when it is not the chief reason for referral. The prevalence of both memory impairment and health conditions that affect memory abilities increase with age. The CVLT is frequently used to assess older adults not only to identify memory impairment but to specify impairments in memory processes that can help differentiate diagnoses and develop targeted interventions.

It is important to assess for sensory impairments and other common physical problems when testing older adults. Many of these can be easily accommodated for if they are identified prior to testing. Hearing impairment is particularly common and may compromise results on CVLT. Older adults who frequently ask for repetitions, speak loudly, complain about outside noise, mishear you, fail to respond to questions, or focus intently on you when you are speaking may have hearing impairments. Remind examinees to bring and wear assistive hearing devices during testing. If you frequently test older adults, you may want to keep a portable amplification device in your testing room for use when hearing aids are not used or are forgotten. In extreme situations, it may not be possible to obtain valid results with the CVLT.

Prior to testing, obtain information on the examinee's health and medication status to help plan the test session. Current medications or recent changes in medication are important as many medications affect arousal levels, both positively and negatively. If an examinee is taking medication that may cause drowsiness, plan testing time around medication to optimize the examinee's performance during the day. This information is often available through care providers or significant others. Medically frail individuals may require more planning to ensure breaks are given appropriately and don't interfere with delay times or administration of the CVLT trials. If CVLT is being administered as part of a longer battery, plan breaks or testing across multiple sessions to complete all measures. However, CVLT must be administered within the same testing session. Use of the Short/Brief Form may also help shorten overall administration time with these individuals. See Rapid Reference 2.2 for guidance on how to select which form to use. For more information on the assessment of older adults, see Edelstein and Koven (2011),

Lezak, Howieson, Bigler, and Tranel (2012), and/or Lichtenberg, Mast, Carpenter, and Wetherell (2015).

Rapid Reference 2.2

Recommendations for Selection of CVLT Forms

Examinee characteristics	Recommended form
Individuals 16–90 with high memory ability	CVLT3 Standard/Alternate
Individuals 16–90 who need a comprehensive assessment of verbal memory	CVLT3 Standard/Alternate
Individuals 16–90 who need retesting	CVLT3 Standard/Alternate (different form than previous administration)
Individuals 16–90 for whom fatigue is a concern	CVLT3 Brief
Medically frail individuals 16–90	CVLT3 Brief
Individuals 17–90 with lower memory ability or who are cognitively impaired	CVLT3 Standard/Alternate
Individuals 16 with lower memory ability or who are cognitively impaired	CVLT C
Individuals 8–15	CVLT C
Individuals 16–89 who are participating in longitudinal research	CVLT-II or CVLT 3 form used in the study

RULES OF ADMINISTRATION

All of the administration directions and word lists for the CVLT are provided in the manual and on the record forms. No stimuli are presented to the examinee, all administration is presented orally by the examiner. Correct responses for the recognition conditions are presented in bold on the record forms. Any unusual behavior that occurs during testing can be noted in the margins of the record form or on a separate piece of paper. The CVLT manuals provide examples of recording and detailed scoring information.

Recording Responses

You must record all responses made during each trial of the CVLT. It is important to accurately record all responses in the same order provided by the examinee, as accurate classification of responses is needed to obtain the process scores. You may find it helpful to use shorthand (e.g., recording the first three letters of a word) during administration, particularly when an examinee responds quickly. If you utilize this approach, make sure to fill in the complete response after testing to ensure accurate scoring. Audio recording the administration is also useful in ensuring accurate capture of responses. Because scoring is not completed during administration, it is important to capture each response accurately on every trial.

Some standard abbreviations may be helpful to accurately capture responses. Rapid Reference 2.3 lists some common abbreviations that may be helpful for recording responses and behaviors during the administration of CVLT. These abbreviations will reflect the testing session, capturing not only the examinee's responses but also standardized prompts and queries given during administration. For example, for each trial on CVLT, a single prompt for more responses is given to elicit further responses. This prompt should be indicated with a P on the record form to note that the prompt was given.

Rapid Reference 2.3

Common Abbreviations Used in Standardized Testing

Abbreviation	Meaning
P	Prompt given
Q	Query given
SC	Self-corrected
DK	Don't Know
NR	No response

Occasionally, an examinee may not recall any responses during a trial, responding with *I don't know* or not responding at all. If this occurs, record DK and score 0 for the trial. If this occurs during a recognition trial, provide the specified prompt and if no response is made record a DK next to the item and code the refusal as a No response on Yes/No recognition or as an error on forced-choice recognition.

CAUTION 2.4

Recording DK and NR Responses

Condition	Recording
All Recall Trials	Record DK or NR
Long-Delay Yes/No Recognition & CVLT-C Long-Delay Recognition	Record DK or NR but code as No
Long-Delay Forced-Choice Recognition	Record DK or NR

Repetition of responses by an examinee within a trial requires special attention. If it is clear that a response is intended as a response, it should be recorded along with other responses. If it is clear that the response is a self-cue and is not intended as a response, do not record the self-cue as a response. If it is not clear whether a repetition is a response or a self-cue, ask the examinee to clarify and record as appropriate.

Querying, Prompting, and Repeating

Throughout administration of the CVLT, prompts and queries are used to encourage the examinee to provide all the words they can recall and to clarify responses. Specific rules for prompting examinees and repeating instructions are provided in the CVLT manuals and record forms. Any cues or prompts beyond those provided in the administration directions and guidelines may influence the recall of information. For example, providing prompts that encourage additional responses is appropriate on most trials and may encourage hesitant examinees to respond; however, providing multiple prompts for additional responses within a single trial may cause frustration and irritation and lead to reduced responding. Excessive prompting may also lengthen the testing session, leading to fatigue and lowered performance. The prompts listed in Rapid Reference 2.4 are provided in the standard instructions.

Rapid Reference 2.4

CVLT Prompts

Behavior	Prompt
Examinee indicates they do not recall any more words on a trial or 15 seconds have passed since the last response	Ask, **Anything else?** Say, **See if you can think of any more.**
Examinee asks if a word is from a particular category	Say you cannot answer the question at this time and encourage examinee to take his or her best guess
Responds I don't know or does not respond to an item on a long-delay yes/no recognition trial (CVLT-C recognition)	Say, **I know it may be difficult, but tell me whether you think (insert word) was on the first list.**
Responds I don't know or does not respond to an item on a long-delay forced-choice recognition trial	Say, **I know it may be difficult, but just take your best guess** or **Which one do you think was on the first list?**
Examinee repeats a response during a trial and it is unclear if it a self-cue or a repetition	Ask the examinee if he or she thinks the response had been given before on this trial
Examinee states that they cannot remember any of the words on a trial	Say, **Just give it a try.** Say, **I think you can do it.**

Instructions may be repeated as needed on CVLT to clarify the directions to the examinee. Word lists should never be repeated or reexposed to the examinee. Presenting the words more than once per trial will invalidate the results. Occasionally an examinee may interrupt you as you are reading the word list. If this happens, redirect the examinee and continue to read the list from the point of the interruption. Note this on the record form and consider in interpreting results as this could have an impact on serial clustering on a trial. Recognition items may be repeated if necessary but note excessive requests for repetition as this may indicate hearing difficulties or extreme attentional difficulties.

DON'T FORGET 2.1

General Administration Tips

Prior to administering CVLT, familiarize yourself with the test administration and materials.

Prior to testing, remind the examinee to bring any hearing assistive devices to testing. Ask about any hearing difficulties that may affect performance.

Plan your test session ahead of time. This includes planning tasks to administer during the delay times, needed modifications or accommodations, and frequency of breaks.

During administration, maintain attention to the examinee's behavior and needs. Provide direction and feedback as needed to elicit the examinee's best effort throughout testing.

Prompt for additional responses when the examinee completes their initial recall on each trial.

Provide encouragement by praising effort, not accuracy. Do not provide feedback on any trials or items.

Prompt for the examinee to guess if they say *I don't know* or don't respond to an item in one of the recognition trials.

Record all responses during testing and note any unusual behaviors or responses. You can evaluate all the responses later as needed.

SPECIFIC TRIAL ADMINISTRATION GUIDELINES

The administration of each task is briefly described within this section, but a thorough review of the administration guidelines in the manuals is suggested to ensure full knowledge of all the nuances of each CVLT edition. Within the detailed description of each task, behaviors to watch for during administration of that task are noted. Appendix A provides a checklist of CVLT administrative procedures for each edition. This checklist may be helpful for individuals first learning the instrument or teaching administration of the CVLT to graduate students or other examiners.

Learning Trials (All CVLT Editions and Forms)

Each CVLT edition and form has four to five learning trials. For each trial, read the word list at a rate of one word every 1–1.5 seconds. Ensure the examinee understands the task and answer any questions before reading the word list on Trial 1. Do not tell the examinee the total number of times you will read the list or that the list will be presented multiple times during Trial 1. If the examinee interrupts you during reading of the word list or begins reciting words before the list is completed, redirect them and continue reading the list beginning with the word where the disruption occurred.

Following the presentation of the word list for each trial, the examinee should verbally recite as many words from the list as they can recall. Record each response verbatim in the order recited by the examinee. If an examinee's response is unclear, you may ask for clarification. If a response is repeated, it is important to determine if the response was intended as a response or as a self-cue. If it is not clear during administration, ask the examinee whether the response was intended using the specified prompt. Record all intended responses for scoring following administration. In addition, mark *I don't know* responses and no responses when appropriate. Although you can use shorthand during administration, be sure to write in complete responses upon completion of administration as scoring is dependent upon accurate recording. If an examinee does not make a response for 15 seconds or indicates they have finished recalling words, prompt once for any additional responses. This prompt is provided only once per trial.

Occasionally, an examinee will repeat words immediately after you read a word. If this occurs on only one or two items, note the behavior but do not interrupt or address the behavior. In these instances, it is okay to nod in affirmation if the examinee repeats the word as a question. However, if the examinee repeats every word after presentation throughout a learning trial. After presenting the list and administering the recall trial, it is appropriate to address the behavior. Prompt the examinee not to repeat each word after you say it but wait until after the entire list has been presented. Note this behavior as it could indicate poor understanding of the task or poor encoding strategies.

The learning trials provide a detailed look at attention and learning processes key in learning and recalling verbal information. Behavioral observations made during the trials can help interpret results. For example, if an examinee mishears a word during initial trials but corrects the response later in the learning trials, it could indicate hearing problems that may result in lower scores on the initial trials. This could suggest an alternate interpretation for lower Trial 1 scores and possibly Total Intrusions scores than memory difficulties.

Possible Behavioral Observations During the Learning Trials

- Interrupting the presentation of the word list to begin a response.
- Recitation of items during presentation of the list, quietly rehearsing or lip movement that suggests internal repetition.
- Recalling a phonetically similar word to one presented in the list.
- Varying attention during the reading of the word list as indicated by glancing around the room or other distracted behaviors.
- Varying attention across the presentation of the list or across learning trials.
- Grouping words by semantic category or attempting to recall the words in a specific order.

- Frequent self-cueing during recall.
- Only recalling words not said on previous trials.
- Recalling the same words across the trials or recalling the same words as the previous trial along with 1–2 more.
- Expressions of frustration or confusion.
- Hesitations, restarts, or frequent self-corrections that indicate he or she has difficulty beginning, inhibiting, or monitoring responses.
- Poor motivation or stating he or she cannot recall anything.

Interference Trial: List B (CVLT-II and CVLT3 Standard and Alternate Forms, CVLT-C)

The Standard and Alternate forms of the CVLT-II and CVLT3 and the CVLT-C include an interference trial following the learning trials. Read the interference word list at the same rate as in the learning trials, one word every 1–1.5 seconds. If the examinee interrupts you during reading of the word list or begins reciting words before the list is completed, redirect them and continue reading the list beginning with the word where the disruption occurred. Following the presentation of the interference word list, the examinee should verbally recite as many words from the list as they can recall. Record each response verbatim in the order recited by the examinee; use the same recording procedures, prompts, and queries as in the learning trials. Record all intended responses for scoring following administration.

The interference trial provides a second immediate recall trial but also serves as interference for recall of the initial word list. Comparison of scores on the first trials of the two word lists provide information on the impact of proactive interference on immediate recall. Behavioral observations made during the trials can help interpret results, just as in the learning trials.

Possible Behavioral Observations During the Interference Trial

- Interrupting the presentation of the word list to begin a response.
- Recitation of items during presentation of the list, quiet rehearsing or lip movement that suggests internal repetition.
- Recalling a phonetically similar word to one presented in the list.
- Varying attention during the reading of the word list as indicated by glancing around the room or other distracted behaviors.
- Frequent self-cueing during recall.
- Recalling words from the initial list.
- Grouping words by semantic categories or attempting to recall words in a specific order.
- Expressions of frustration or confusion.
- Hesitations, restarts, or frequent self-corrections that indicate he or she has difficulty beginning, inhibiting, or monitoring responses.
- Poor motivation or stating he or she cannot recall anything.

30-Second Distractor Task (CVLT-II Short Form, CVLT3 Brief Form)

For the Short Form and Brief Form, an interference trial is not given. Instead a 30-seconds distractor task is administered to prevent the examinee from reciting the words following completion of the four learning trials. The examinee counts backward from 100 for 30 seconds. Do not provide any feedback or corrections on the performance of this task, although you should note any difficulties the examinee exhibits. Stop the examinee and proceed to the short-delay free-recall task once 30-seconds have passed. Behavioral observations made during the interference task may provide insight into difficulties the examinee has outside of recall or provide insight into strategies the examinee uses to retain information through distracting tasks.

Possible Behavioral Observations During the Distraction Task

- Making frequent reverse counting errors or counting forwards.
- Responding consistently for 30 seconds.
- Failing to continue counting for 30 seconds.
- Continuing to count backwards after being instructed to stop.
- Recitation of word list words during the distraction task.
- Expressions of frustration or confusion.
- Hesitations, restarts, or frequent self-corrections that indicate the examinee has difficulty beginning, inhibiting, or monitoring responses.
- Refusal to complete the reverse counting task.
- Poor motivation or stating he or she cannot count backwards.

Short-Delay Free Recall (All Forms)

Each CVLT edition has a short-delay free-recall trial following either the interference word list or the distractor task. The word list is not reread to the examinee. The examinee verbally recites as many words from the original word list as they can recall. Record each response verbatim in the order recited by the examinee; use the same recording procedures, prompts, and queries as in the learning and interference trials. Record all intended responses for scoring following administration.

The short-delay free-recall trial describes the examinees ability to recall verbal information following an interference task. Comparison of scores on the final learning trial and the short-delay recall trial provides information on the impact of interference on immediate recall. Behavioral observations made during the short-delay free recall can help interpret results, just as in the earlier trials.

Possible Behavioral Observations During the Short-Delay Free-Recall Trial

- Recalling words from both lists.
- Grouping words by semantic category.
- Recalling a phonetically similar word to one presented in the list.
- Frequent self-cueing during recall.
- Expressions of frustration or confusion.

- Hesitations, restarts, or frequent self-corrections that indicate he or she has difficulty beginning, inhibiting, or monitoring responses.
- Poor motivation or stating he or she cannot recall anything.

Short-Delay Cued Recall (CVLT-II and CVLT3 Standard and Alternate Forms, CVLT-C)

On the Standard and Alternate forms of each CVLT edition, a short-delay cued-recall trial follows the short-delay free task. The word list is not reread to the examinee. Provide each semantic category and ask the examinee to verbally recall the words from the original list that were in that category. Occasionally, an examinee may ask what a particular category name means. If this occurs, provide a general description of the category, as described in the respective manual. Record each response verbatim in the order recited by the examinee; use the same recording procedures, prompts, and queries as in the earlier trials. In addition to these prompts, if the examinee does not recall all the words from the original list that are in the semantic category presented, prompt the examinee once and record the prompt on the record form. This cue is given once per semantic category; do not provide this cue if all words from the category are recalled. If the examinee asks whether a recalled word is from the current category, say you cannot tell him or her and encourage them to take his or her best guess.

CAUTION 2.5

Do not inform the examinee that he or she will be asked to recall the word list again after a delay.

Record all intended responses, including responses that are not from the current category, for scoring following administration. Present all appropriate semantic categories for the form (four for CVLT-II and CVLT3 Standard and Alternate Forms; three for the CVLT-C) during the cued-recall trial. Do not inform the examinee that he or she will be asked to recall the words again after a delay.

The short-delay cued-recall trial provides examinees with the semantic categories for the words in the word list. This provides cues for clustering words for recall and provides a strategy that may aid in recall. Prior to this trial all recall performances were reliant on the examinees strategies for recalling information. Comparison of scores on the free- and cued-recall trials provides information on the impact of introducing recall strategies or providing structure on recall. Behavioral observations made during the short-delay cued recall can help interpret results, just as in the earlier trials.

Possible Behavioral Observations During the Short-Delay Cued-Recall Trial

- Asking for definition of a category.
- Recalling words from the list that are not in the current semantic category.
- Recalling words from the interference list that are in the current semantic category.
- Recalling intrusions from earlier trials.
- Saying words from the semantic category that are not from either list.
- Recalling a phonetically similar word to one presented in the list.

- Frequent self-cueing during recall.
- Expressions of frustration or confusion.
- Hesitations, restarts, or frequent self-corrections that indicate he or she has difficulty beginning, inhibiting, or monitoring responses.
- Poor motivation or stating he or she cannot recall anything.

Delay (All Forms)

Before administering any further recall trials, administer unrelated visual or nonverbal tasks for a designated period of time (15–25 min for CVLT-II and CVLT3 Standard and Alternate Forms; approximately 20 min for CVLT-C; roughly 10 min for CVLT-II Brief Form and CVLT3 Short Form). While you may go slightly longer on the delay time if you are completing a task or engaged in conversation, you must not administer the delayed trials until the minimum amount of time has passed. The minimum time must pass in order to ensure adequate time for consolidation and memory decay to occur. There are not any specific tasks that are required to be administered during this delay time period but the full delay time should be observed prior to the delay recall trials. Once the delay time has passed, proceed to the long-delay free-recall task. Behavioral observations made during the delay period are likely related to the types of tasks selected and administered by you. Therefore, the list of behavioral observations made during the delay time is limited to behaviors that the examinee may be engaging in during the delay to retain the word lists. Because the examinee is not informed that they will be recalling the word list again, many behaviors related to retention of information will not occur. However, any observations related to recall of the word lists can help with the interpretation of performance on the delayed recall trials.

Possible Behavioral Observations During the Distraction Task

- Recitation of word list words during the delay tasks.
- Quietly rehearsing the word lists or lip movement that suggests internal repetition of the word lists.
- Slower than expected performance on the tasks administered during the delay period due to rehearsing the word lists.
- Making references to words from the list during conversation (e.g., *I remembered umbrella every time.*)

Long-Delay Free Recall (All Forms)

After at least the minimum amount of delay time has elapsed, administer the long-delay free-recall trial. The word list is not reread to the examinee. The examinee verbally recites as many words from the original word list as they can recall. Because the examinee was not told he or she would have to recall the list again, examinees may verbalize confusion, mild anger, or frustration that he or she was not told to remember the words. You may address these feelings briefly but proceed to the free-recall trial as soon as reasonable. Record each response verbatim in the order recited by the examinee; use the same recording procedures, prompts, and queries as in the learning and short-delay recall trials. Record all intended responses for scoring following administration.

The long-delay free-recall trial describes the examinee's ability to recall verbal information following a delay of several minutes during which nonrelated tasks are completed. Comparison of scores on the short-delay free-recall trial and the long-delay free-recall trial provides information on the impact of time passage on recall. Behavioral observations made during the long-delay free-recall trial can help with the interpretation of results, just as in the earlier trials.

Possible Behavioral Observations During the Long-Delay Free-Recall Trial

- Recalling words from both lists.
- Grouping words by semantic category or trying to recall words in a specific order.
- Recalling a phonetically similar word to one presented in the list.
- Recalling an intrusion from the earlier trials.
- Frequent self-cueing during recall.
- Expressions of frustration or confusion.
- Hesitations, restarts, or frequent self-corrections that indicate he or she has difficulty beginning, inhibiting, or monitoring responses.
- Poor motivation or stating he or she cannot recall anything.

Long-Delay Cued Recall (All Forms)

Immediately following long-delay free recall, administer the long-delay cued-recall trial. The word list is not reread to the examinee. Provide each semantic category and ask the examinee to verbally recall the words from the original list that were in that category. If the examinee asks what a particular category name means, provide a general description of the category, as described in the respective manual. Record each response verbatim in the order recited by the examinee; use the same recording procedures, prompts, and queries as in the earlier trials. In addition to these prompts, if the examinee does not recall all the words from the original list that are in the semantic category presented, prompt the examinee once and record the prompt on the record form. This cue is given once per semantic category; do not provide this cue if all words from the category are recalled. If the examinee asks whether a recalled word is from the current category, say you cannot tell him or her and encourage them to take his or her best guess.

Record all intended responses, including responses that are not from the current category, for scoring following administration. Present all appropriate semantic categories for the form (four for CVLT-II and CVLT3 Standard and Alternate Forms; three for the CVLT-II Brief Form, CVLT3 Short Form, and CVLT-C) during the long-delay cued-recall trial.

The long-delay cued-recall trial provides examinees with the semantic categories for the words in the word list. This reinforces the cues for clustering words semantically and provides a strategy that may aid in recall. Comparison of scores on the free- and cued delayed-recall trials provides information on the impact of introducing recall strategies or providing structure on recall. Behavioral observations made during the long-delay cued recall can help interpret results, just as in the earlier trials.

Possible Behavioral Observations During the Short-Delay Cued-Recall Trial

- Recalling intrusions from earlier trials.
- Asking for a description or definition of the semantic category.
- Recalling words from the list that are not in the current semantic category.
- Recalling words from the interference list that are in the current semantic category.
- Saying words from the semantic category that are not from either list.
- Recalling a phonetically similar word to one presented in the list.
- Frequent self-cueing during recall.
- Expressions of frustration or confusion.
- Hesitations, restarts, or frequent self-corrections that indicate he or she has difficulty beginning, inhibiting, or monitoring responses.
- Poor motivation or stating he or she cannot recall anything.

Long-Delay Yes/No Recognition (All Forms)

Following the long-delay free- and cued-recall trials, administer the long-delay yes/no recognition trial. Recognition memory allows you to observe whether an examinee can identify the words correctly when not required to retrieve the information and express it. Most examinees find recognition easier than recall. For each item in this trial, read the word clearly and ask the examinee to respond yes or no to indicate whether it was a word from the original list. Be sure not to use different inflection or provide cues as to the correct response to an item. The examinee says *Yes* if the word was one he or she thought was from the original list and *No* if the word was not one he or she recalled from the original list. If the examinee responds *I don't know* or refuses to answer an item, prompt the examinee with the suggested prompts to guess or reread the instruction. Circle Y for *Yes* responses and N for *No* responses, *I don't know* responses, or refusals.

Possible Behavioral Observations During Long-Delay Yes/No Recognition Trial

- Frequent refusals to guess.
- Responding with all yes or all no responses.
- Responding with a clear pattern of yes and no responses.
- Asking for frequent repetitions of the words.
- Self-talk during responding.
- Expressions of frustration or confusion.
- Hesitations, restarts, multiple responses to a single item, or frequent self-corrections that indicate he or she has difficulty beginning, inhibiting, or monitoring responses.
- Poor motivation or refusal to answer any item.

Long-Delay Forced-Choice Recognition (All Forms of the CVLT-II and CVLT3)

Forced-Choice Recognition is the only optional trial on the CVLT. If you choose to administer this trial, you should wait approximately 10 min after administering the Yes/No Recognition trial on the Standard or Alternate Forms or approximately 5 min after administering the Yes/No Recognition trial on the Brief and Short Forms. This delay should be filled with nonverbal tasks, just as in the earlier delay. Ensure this delay does not run shorter than the minimum delay time provided in the manuals (7 min on Standard/Alternate forms, 3 min on Brief/Short forms). Unlike the Yes/No Recognition trial, the Forced-Choice Recognition trial is a performance validity measure with most examinees obtaining near perfect scores. Poor performance on this trial suggests the need for further evaluation of overall performance validity, except in examinees with severe memory deficits. Additional performance validity measures are suggested when raw scores are low.

For each item in this recognition trial, read two words and ask the examinee to select the word he or she recalls from the original list. The distractor or incorrect words for this task are not from the interference list, the yes/no recognition trial, or any other presented trial. In addition, none of the distractor words are from the same semantic categories provided to the examinee during the cued-recall trials. Be sure not to use different inflection or provide cues as to the correct response to an item. If the examinee responds *I don't know*, refuses to answer an item, or hesitates, provide the prompt to guess or clarify the instruction. Circle the word selected by the examinee. If the examinee fails to respond, selects both responses and fails to clarify, or says *I don't know*, score the item as an error (0 points).

Possible Behavioral Observations During Long-Delay Forced-Choice Recognition Trial

- Frequent refusals to guess.
- Responding to all items with only the first or second word options.
- Asking for frequent repetitions of the words.
- Self-talk during responding.
- Expressions of frustration or confusion.
- Hesitations, restarts, multiple responses to a single item, or frequent self-corrections that indicate he or she has difficulty beginning, inhibiting, or monitoring responses.
- Poor motivation or refusal to answer any item.

DON'T FORGET 2.2

Common Examiner Mistakes

Learning Trials

- Reading the word list too quickly or too slowly
- Stopping administration and repeating items if the examinee appears to have become inattentive
- Repeating items at the examinee's request
- Failing to record all responses in the order in which the examinee recalls the words.
- Failing to prompt for additional responses after 15 seconds of no response or when the examinee states he or she can't recall any more information

- Failing to administer all learning trials, even if the examinee recalls all words on an early trial
- Providing feedback during the recall on any trial

Interference List

- Reading the word list too quickly or too slowly
- Stopping administration and repeating items if the examinee appears to have become inattentive
- Repeating items at the examinee's request
- Failing to record all responses in the order in which the examinee recalls the words
- Failing to prompt for additional responses after 15 seconds of no response or when the examinee states he or she can't recall any more information

Short-Delay and Long-Delay Free Recall

- Representing the word list
- Failing to record all responses in the order in which the examinee recalls the words
- Failing to prompt for additional responses after 15 seconds of no response or when the examinee states he or she can't recall any more information
- Providing feedback during the recall trial
- Administering the delayed condition before the appropriate time has elapsed

Short-Delay and Long-Delay Cued Recall

- Representing the word list
- Failing to present all the semantic categories
- Failing to provide the generic category description when asked
- Providing feedback to an examinee if they are unsure of whether a word belongs to a specific category
- Failing to record all responses in the order in which the examinee recalls the words
- Failing to prompt for additional responses if the examinee does not provide all the correct responses for a category
- Providing feedback during the recall trial
- Administering the delayed condition before the appropriate time has elapsed

Long-Delay Yes/No Recognition

- Using nonneutral intonation when reading the word for an item
- Providing feedback during an item
- Recording an *I don't know* response or refusal as missing
- Failing to prompt the examinee to guess if they fail to respond or say I don't know

Long-Delay Forced-Choice Recognition

- Administering immediately after Long-Delay Yes/No Recognition, without waiting the appropriate delay interval

(*continued*)

- Using nonneutral intonation when reading the words for an item
- Providing feedback during an item
- Recording an *I don't know* response or refusal as missing
- Failing to prompt the examinee to guess if they fail to respond or say I don't know

TEST YOURSELF

1. During conversation prior to testing, your examinee rubs her arms, shifts in her chair, and keeps her arms tightly crossed. You:

(a) write these behaviors down to use in interpreting results.
(b) ask if she is comfortable and make adjustments if needed.
(c) stop the assessment and reschedule.
(d) keep talking; she will tell you if she is uncomfortable.

2. In preparing for an evaluation, you find out that the examinee has multiple chronic medical issues and tires easily. The referral question requires that the CVLT be given as part of a longer battery of tests so you plan to see the examinee across multiple test sessions. What must you do to ensure that all the CVLT scores are available and valid after completing all of the instruments in the battery?

(a) Administer all desired trials of the CVLT within a single session and ensure the appropriate time delays between trials.
(b) Administer the CVLT and all other desired memory measures in a single session, the impact of fatigue should be assessed as part of the evaluation.
(c) Administer the learning and short-delay recall trials during the first session and the delayed tasks during the second session.
(d) Don't administer CVLT as part of the battery; memory is not an important construct in a case with chronic medical issues.

**3. All administration information is found on the CVLT record form.
True or False**

4. As you are reading the word list during the learning trials, you notice that the examinee is glancing around the room and does not seem to be paying attention. What should you do?

(a) Stop administration of the word list, redirect the examinee to the task, and restart the trial from the beginning.
(b) Stop administration of the word list, discontinue the CVLT, and reschedule the test session for when the examinee may be more attentive.
(c) Complete administration of the word list on the current trial, including recall, and redirect the examinee to the task at the beginning of the next trial.

(d) Redirect the examinee and complete administration of the word list from the next unpresented word in the list; note the behavior on the record form and then continue with the next trial.

5. The CVLT is a comprehensive assessment of all processes involved in learning and memory of all information.
True or False

6. Words can be repeated at the examinee's request only on the learning trials.
True or False

7. Which trial is optional on the CVLT-II and CVLT3?
(a) Learning Trial 5
(b) Short-Delay Cued Recall
(c) Long-Delay Yes/No Recognition
(d) Long-Delay Forced-Choice Recognition

8. Which form of the CVLT does not have an Interference Trial?
(a) CVLT-C Standard Form
(b) CVLT3 Short Form
(c) CVLT-II Alternate Form
(d) CVLT3 Standard Form

9. When do you discontinue administration of the learning trials in CVLT?
(a) Do not discontinue; administer all of the learning trials.
(b) Following correct recall of all the words in two consecutive trials
(c) If the examinee recalls less than four words in a trial
(d) When the examinee does not recall more words than the previous trial

10. Which of the following is appropriate during administration of the CVLT?
(a) Telling the examinee that they have already said a word when asked
(b) Praising the examinee for recalling correct words
(c) Prompting for additional responses once per recall trial
(d) Reading the word list after the Interference trial or Distractor task

11. Following completion of the short-delay cued-recall trial, inform the examinee that they will be asked to recall the words later and proceed with nonverbal testing during the delay interval.
True or False

12. You are scheduled to evaluate a 16-year-old examinee who is seeking accommodations on college admissions testing to help compensate for difficulties he has experienced on standardized schoolwide assessments. Given his age, all three editions of the CVLT are available. Which edition of the CVLT is most appropriate for this examinee?
(a) CVLT-C
(b) CVLT-II Standard Form
(c) CVLT3 Standard Form
(d) CVLT3 Short Form

13. You are scheduled to evaluate a 73-year-old examinee who is participating in a longitudinal study on memory. The study has used the CVLT-II in the three previous assessments, alternating between the Standard and Alternate forms with the Standard form administered most recently. Which edition is most appropriate for this examinee?

(a) CVLT3 Short Form

(b) CVLT-II Standard Form

(c) CVLT3 Standard Form

(d) CVLT-II Alternate Form

14. You are planning to assess an examinee with hearing difficulties. Which of the following approaches would best suit this situation?

(a) Provide the written words of the word list during administration to ensure accurate understanding of the words.

(b) Administer the short form only as there are fewer words to hear on this list and it will cause less frustration for the examinee.

(c) Ensure the examinee is wearing any amplification devices and clearly enunciate each word; note any recalled words that indicate mishearing of the information.

(d) Do not use the CVLT as it is not clear that the examinee will hear all the words correctly.

Answers: 1. b, 2. a, 3. True, 4. c, 5. False, 6. False, 7. d, 8. b, 9. a; 10. c; 11. False; 12. c; 13. d; 14. c

Three

HOW TO SCORE THE CVLT-C, CVLT-II, AND CVLT3

Although the administration of California Verbal Learning Test (CVLT) is relatively straightforward and easy to learn, completing the scoring is more complex and may take longer to learn. However, understanding how the scores are derived is critical to accurately interpreting them. The most efficient and error-free approach to scoring is to use the digital scoring software. Several scores are available only through the scoring software due to the methods required to derive them. However, because digital scoring is not feasible in all situations and it is important to understand how scores are derived even if you use the scoring software, this chapter breaks down scoring on the CVLT, from classifying responses to deriving standard scores. It includes directions on how to hand score the primary scores and some process scores. The methods used to derive all available scores are described in the appropriate CVLT manual. If you are using only the primary recall and recognition trial scores, hand scoring will require approximately 10 min to complete. To derive all the scores possible through hand scoring, approximately 30–45 min are required depending upon the length and complexity of the examinee's responses and your familiarity with scoring. If you use different editions of the CVLT, pay particular attention to calculation differences across editions.

Throughout this chapter, figures are presented to illustrate key information required to appropriately classify and score responses. In order to maintain test security and protect copyright, these examples use fake word lists. These lists are used for illustrative purposes only and are not intended as alternate word lists to be used within CVLT.

CLASSIFYING RESPONSES ON RECALL TRIALS

The first step in scoring CVLT, either digitally or by hand, is to classify each response *within each trial* as either correct or incorrect. Incorrect responses are further classified as repetitions (perseverations on CVLT-C) or intrusions. Repetitions are either correct or incorrect words that are repeated at least once during a trial. Intrusions are responses that are not words from the current list. There is a column on the record form to classify each response as correct (C), Repetition (R), or Intrusion (I). On CVLT-C, repetitions are classified as perseverations and identified with a P. All responses, even those given after a prompt or query, are classified and included in scoring. For the CVLT3, only the first 20 responses given during a free-recall trial and only the first 8 responses given in response to a semantic cue within a cued-recall trial are classified and used in scoring. Detailed descriptions of the various classifications are provided next; refer to Figure 3.1 throughout this section for examples of each type of responses.

For classifying responses in Q-global or Q-interactive, responses that are directly selected from the word lists are automatically scored appropriately. For intrusions, you will need to classify each response within the scoring system using the same guidance guidelines as hand scoring.

Correct Responses

On all trials, singular or plural versions of a correct word are considered correct. Synonyms are not considered correct responses. Any acceptable alternate correct responses for a list word, such as common acronyms or abbreviations, are listed in the respective manual.

Learning Trials: For each trial, any response that is the first recall of a word from List A is classified as correct.

Interference (List B) Trial: Any response that is the first recall of a word from List B is classified as correct. Any words recalled from List A are incorrect.

Short-Delay and Long-Delay Free-Recall Trials: Any response that is the first recall of a word from List A is classified as correct. Any words recalled from List B are incorrect.

Short-Delay and Long-Delay Cued-Recall Trials: The cued-recall trials include four category cues. On CVLT-C and CVLT-II, any response that is the first recall of a word from List A and is recalled during the related semantic cue is classified as correct. Any words recalled from List B are incorrect, even if they are from the same semantic category. On CVLT3, the first recall of a word from List A is correct, even if it is first recalled during the wrong semantic cue (see Figure 3.2).

> **CAUTION 3.1**
>
> Correct response classification differs across CVLT editions on Cued-Recall Trials.
>
> CVLT-C and CVLT-II: first recall of a word from List A and is recalled during the related semantic cue is classified as correct
>
> CVLT3: first recall of a word from List A is correct, even if it is recalled during the wrong semantic cue

Repetitions (Perseverations on CVLT-C)

All Learning, Interference, and Free-Recall Trials: For each trial, any response that has been previously said **within the same trial**; both correct responses and intrusions can be repeated. Responses that were given as self-cueing (see Chapter 2) should not be included in the responses or classified as repetitions.

> **DON'T FORGET 3.1**
>
> Repetitions are called perseverations on the CVLT-C.

Fake List A	**Trial 1**		**Trial 2**		**Trial 3**		**Trial 4**		**Trial 5**	
sofa	*purple*	*C*	*baseball*	*C*	*ankle*	*C*	*hockey*	*C*	*hockey*	*C*
purple	*chairs*	*C*	*brown*	*C*	*thumb*	*C*	*sofa*	*C*	*bowling*	*C*
nose	*nightstand*	*C*	*purple*	*C*	*bowling*	*C*	*chairs*	*C*	*nose*	*C*
baseball	*thumb*	*C*	*hockey*	*C*	*nightstand*	*C*	*ankle*	*C*	*bureau*	*C*
yellow	*bowling*	*C*	*chairs*	*C*	*chairs*	*C*	*brown*	*C*	*chairs*	*C*
chair	*sofa*	*C*	*yellow*	*C*	*hockey*	*C*	*orange*	*C*	*archery*	*C*
archery	*purple*	*R*	*brown*	*R*	*yellow*	*C*	*thumb*	*C*	*hockey*	*R*
arm	*bed*	*I*	*bed*	*I*	*chair*	*R*	*nightstand*	*C*	*arm*	*C*
bureau	~~*purple*~~		*nightstand*	*C*	*bed*	*I*	*sofa*	*R*	*ear*	*I*
hockey	*P*		*red*	*I*	*P*		*purple*	*C*	*ankle*	*C*
orange	*apple*	*I*	*pig*	*I*	*ear*	*I*	*P*		*brown*	*C*
thumb	*couch*	*I*	*P*		*bed*	*R/I*			*purple*	*C*
bowling			*telephone*	*I*					*P*	
nightstand										
ankle										
brown										

Fake List B	**Recall**	
pig	*grey*	*C*
grey	*pink*	*C*
ear	*tie*	*C*
dress	*ankle*	*I*
pink	*head*	*I*
gazelle	*shoulder*	*C*
tie	*knee*	*I*
elbow	*monkey*	*C*
hamster	*car*	*I*
socks	*P*	
red	couch	*I*
neck		
suspenders		
monkey		
shoulder		
silver		

Figure 3.1. Scoring sample trials 1–5 and interference trial.

Furniture		Colors		Body parts		Sports	
chair	C	*purple*	C	*thumb*	C	*baseball*	C
bed	I	*yellow*	C	*ankle*	C	*soccer*	I
sofa	C	*red*	I	*orange*	C[a]	*P*	
P		*P*		*nose*	C		
				P			

[a]Note that this would be an intrusion on CVLT-II but is a correct response on CVLT3.

Figure 3.2. Scoring sample short-delay cued recall trial.

If a singular word is given and then repeated as a plural, or vice versa, the second response is classified as a repetition. Repeated intrusions are classified as both an intrusion and a repetition (record I/R on the record form). In Figure 3.1, purple is repeated twice on Trial 1 so the second repetition is crossed out and not counted in the repetitions total; bed is an intrusion and is repeated on Trial 3 so the repetition is classified as both a repetition and an intrusion.

Short-Delay and Long-Delay Cued-Recall Trials: The cued-recall trials include four category cues. On CVLT-C and CVLT-II, any response that was previously recalled within the responses for a single semantic cue is classified as a repetition (perseveration). On CVLT3, any response that was previously recalled during any semantic cue is classified as a repetition. In Figure 3.2, orange is recalled following the body parts cue. On CVLT-C and CVLT-II, *orange* would not be counted as correct within the cued-recall trial but is classified as an intrusion, so Total Correct for the trial is 10. On CVLT3, *orange* would be counted as correct within the cued-recall trial even though it was recalled under an unrelated cue, so Total Correct for the trial is 11.

Intrusions

Classify each response that is not on the current recall list as an intrusion. Intrusions can be classified as category (semantically related) and noncategory (semantically unrelated) intrusions. Category intrusions are responses that belong to one of the semantic categories from either list presented (note that during the learning trials List B has not been presented so category intrusions are only those words related to the semantic categories for the first list). Noncategory intrusions are responses that do not belong to any of the semantic categories presented prior to the intrusion. Intrusions on Trials 1–5 are considered noncategory intrusions if they do belong to the categories in the original list.

In Figure 3.1, *ear* is given as a response in Trial 3, which is an intrusion even though it appears on List B; *ear* is a category intrusion because the body parts category has been introduced. Alternatively, *pig* is given as a response in Trial 2; this is an intrusion but is a noncategory intrusion because the category of animals has not yet been introduced.

Category intrusions can further be broken down into novel words not presented to the examinee, synonyms or subordinates of a presented list word, or cross-list intrusions, a word recalled from a presented list that is not the current target list. Note that subtypes of category intrusions should be counted as both category intrusions and the subtype intrusion. In Figure 2.1, *couch* in Trial 1 is a synonym/subordinate intrusion because it is not a word in the list but is a synonym for sofa. Be careful in categorizing across-list intrusions; during the learning trials there are no across-list intrusions as List B has not yet been presented to the examinee. In Figure 2.1, *ear* is given as a response and is classified as a category intrusion; it is not an across list intrusion though because List B has not been presented. Note that across-list intrusions are not available on the Brief/Short Form as only one list is presented. The scoring software will automatically classify across-list intrusions if they are selected from the list but all intrusions entered by you must be classified in order for the error analyses to be completed.

Rapid Reference 3.1

Intrusion Categories Across Editions

Intrusion category (definition)	**CVLT-C**	**CVLT-II**	**CVLT3**
Category Intrusion (novel response that belongs to a presented list category)	Semantically Related intrusion	Category Intrusion	Category Intrusion
Synonym Intrusion (category intrusion that is a synonym of a list word)	Synonym Intrusion	Synonym/ Subordinate intrusion	Synonym/ Subordinate intrusion
Subordinate Intrusion (category intrusion that is a subordinate of a list word)	NA	Synonym/ Subordinate intrusion	Synonym/ Subordinate intrusion
Across-list Intrusion (word recalled from list not currently being recalled)	Cross-trial intrusion	Across-list intrusion	Across-list intrusion
Noncategory Intrusion (novel response that is not from a presented list category)	Semantically unrelated intrusion	Noncategory intrusion	Noncategory intrusion

All Learning Trials: For each trial, mark any response that is not a word from the list (List A) as an intrusion (I). If the word is from one of the categories in the list, categorize it as a category intrusion and indicate whether it is a synonym or subordinate of a word on the list. *There are no across-list intrusions on the learning trials as the interference list has not been presented.* If a response does not belong to one of the categories from the list, categorize it as a noncategory intrusion. If an intrusion is repeated classify it as both an intrusion and a repetition.

Interference Trial: Mark any response that is not a word from the interference list (List B) as an intrusion (I). If the word is from one of the categories from either presented list (both List A and List B), categorize it as a category intrusion. For each category intrusion, indicate whether it is a synonym or subordinate of a word on either list. Also, classify any response from List A as an across-list intrusion. If a response does not belong to one of the categories from either list, categorize it as a non-category intrusion. Any intrusion that is repeated within the trial is classified as both an intrusion and a repetition.

Short-Delay and Long-Delay Free- and Cued-Recall Trials: Mark any response that is not a word from the original list (List A) as an intrusion (I). If the word is from one of the categories from either presented list (both List A and List B), categorize it as a category intrusion. For each category intrusion, indicate whether it is a synonym or subordinate of a word on either list. Also, classify any response from the interference list (List B) as an across-list intrusion. If a response does not belong to one of the categories from either list, categorize it as a noncategory intrusion. Any intrusion that is repeated within the trial is classified as both an intrusion and a repetition.

DERIVING PRIMARY RAW SCORES

Primary Recall Measures

After all recall responses have been classified, you can calculate the total raw scores for each of the recall trials. This is the first step in deriving the primary normative scores. These raw scores are used to derive some of the process scores as well as the primary normative scores. Although raw scores can provide information on the examinee's performance, particularly on the level of recall across learning and recall trials, normative scores must be derived to place his or her performance within the context of similar-age peers.

For each recall trial, sum the correct responses (C), the repetitions, and the intrusions given within the trial. There is space at the bottom of each trial in the record form to record these totals. The correct responses raw scores for each trial can be transferred to the appropriate box on the summary page of the record form. Note that for the cued-recall trials, all responses to all the cues are included in a single raw score for the cued trial. If an examinee does not respond or says they can not recall any words on a trial, score 0 points for the trial total correct.

Rapid Reference 3.2

Primary Recall Scores Across Editions

Trial	CVLT-C score	CVLT-II score	CVLT3 score
Trial 1 Recall	List A Immediate Free-Recall Trial 1	Trial 1 Free Recall	Trial 1 Correct
Trial 2 Recall	List A Immediate Free-Recall Trial 2	Trial 2 Free Recall	Trial 2 Correct
Trial 3 Recall	List A Immediate Free-Recall Trial 3	Trial 3 Free Recall	Trial 3 Correct
Trial 4 Recall	List A Immediate Free-Recall Trial 4	Trial 4 Free Recall	Trial 4 Correct
Trial 5 Recall	List A Immediate Free-Recall Trial 5	Trial 5 Free Recall	Trial 5 Correct
Learning Trials	Trials 1–5 Total	Trials 1–5 Free-Recall Total Correct	Trials 1–5 Correct (Sum of Scaled Scores)
Interference Trial	List B Trial	List B Free-Recall Correct	List B Correct
Short-Delay Free-Recall Trial	List A Short-Delay Trial Free Recall	Short-Delay Free-Recall Correct	Short-Delay Free-Recall Correct
Short-Delay Cued-Recall Trial	List A Short-Delay Trial Cued Recall	Short-Delay Cued-Recall Correct	Short-Delay Cued-Recall Correct
Long-Delay Free-Recall Trial	List A Long-Delay Trial Free Recall	Long-Delay Free-Recall Correct	Long-Delay Free-Recall Correct
Long-Delay Cued-Recall Trial	List A Long-Delay Trial Cued Recall	Long-Delay Cued-Recall Correct	Long-Delay Cued-Recall Correct

Several raw scores are summed to derive multitrial scores. For CVLT-II and CVLT-C, sum the raw scores of the learning trials to obtain the Trials 1–5 correct raw score. The CVLT3 utilizes a sum of scaled scores for this score and is discussed later in this chapter.

Once the raw scores for correct responses on each trial have been calculated, transfer them to the summary page of the record form if you are hand scoring.

Primary Recognition Measures

Yes/No Recognition produces three primary scores: Total Hits, Total False Positives, and Recognition Discriminability. A hit is the correct identification of a target word from the word list during the recognition task. The recognition items with a correct target word are designated with a T under the Item Type column and by a bolded word and Y response on the record form for the CVLT-II and CVLT3. Sum the total number of Y responses on these items to calculate the Total Hits raw score. For CVLT-C, the recognition items with a target word are designated by the List A column for responses. Sum the total number of checkmarks in the List A column to obtain the Total Hits raw score. Note that if an examinee fails to respond to an item on Yes/No Recognition, it should be scores as a No response.

CAUTION 3.2

Scoring DK and NR Responses

Condition	Recording
All Recall Trials	Score 0 points if no words were recalled for the trial
Long-Delay Yes/No Recognition and CVLT-C Long-Delay Recognition	Score the response as if the examinee said *No*
Long-Delay Forced-Choice Recognition	Score as an error or incorrect response

A false positive is the incorrect identification of a nontarget or distractor word as a correct response during the recognition task (e.g., saying yes to a word not from the correct word list). On the record forms, these items are labeled with an acronym designating the type of distractor word (i.e., BS = list B shared; BSS = List B Superordinate Shared; BN = List B Nonshared; PR(NP) = Prototypical; PS = Neither List Phonetically Similar; UN = Unrelated). For the purposes of deriving the Total False-Positives raw score, these designations are not used. The recognition items without a correct target word are not bolded on the record form for the CVLT-II and CVLT3. Sum the total number of Y responses on the unbolded items to calculate the Total False-Positives raw score. For CVLT-C, the recognition items without a target word are designated by the BS, BSS, BN, NP, and UN columns for responses on the record form. Sum the total number of checkmarks in these columns to obtain the Total False-Positives raw score.

Both total hits and false positives can be heavily influenced by a response bias, such as responding yes to every item. A score can be calculated for response bias but is not easily hand scored and is not considered a primary score. See the respective manuals for information on how to derive the response bias scores. In addition, a measure of discriminability is provided that accounts for accuracy of responding. Discriminability is best measured with the parametric *d'* measure due to the unequal number of targets and distractors on the Yes/No task. However, this measure is difficult to calculate by hand and requires the software to derive; therefore, although it is highly recommended that you use the *d'* measure, for hand scoring a nonparametric approach to deriving a measure of discriminability is also available on the CVLT-C and CVLT3. Discriminability can be derived only with the software on CVLT-II. Although the formula is the same across all forms of the CVLT-C and CVLT3, the standard values are different across editions and forms.

$$\text{CVLT II and CVLT3: } 1 - [(\text{Total False Positives} + (16 - \text{Total Hits}))/48] \times 100$$

$$\text{CVLT} - \text{II and CVLT3 Short/Brief Form: }$$

$$1 - [(\text{Total False Positives} + (9 - \text{Total Hits}))/27] \times 100$$

$$\text{CVLT} - \text{C: } 1 - [(\text{Total False Positives} + (15 - \text{Total Hits}))/45] \times 100$$

Once the raw scores for hits, false positives, and discriminability have been calculated, transfer them to the summary page of the record form if you are hand scoring.

Rapid Reference 3.3

Primary Recognition Scores Across Editions

Trial	**CVLT-C score**	**CVLT-II score**	**CVLT3 score**
Total Hits	Correct Recognition Hits	Yes/No Recognition Hits	Long-Delay Yes/No Recognition Total Hits
Total False Positives	Total False Positives	Yes/No Recognition False Positives	Long-Delay Yes/No Recognition Total False Positives
Recognition Discriminability	Index of Discriminability	Yes/No Recognition Discriminability (*d'*)	Recognition Discriminability (*d'*) Recognition Discriminability Nonparametric
Response Bias	Response Bias Index	Yes/No Response Bias (C)	Response Bias Response Bias Nonparametric

DERIVING STANDARDIZED SCORES FOR PRIMARY MEASURES

The standardized score values differ across CVLT editions. CVLT-C utilizes *T* scores, CVLT-II utilizes *z*-scores and *T* scores, and CVLT3 utilizes scaled scores and index standard scores. Chapter 4 describes the various scores and interpretations. Despite producing different scores, each standardized score is derived in the same manner. Use the calculated raw scores to look up the related standardized score in the normative tables found in the appendix of each CVLT manual. For CVLT-C and CVLT3, the normative tables are presented by age for the appropriate form. For CVLT-II, the normative tables are presented by age and sex. Be sure you are looking at the appropriate table for the demographics of the person being tested. Once you have found the appropriate table, find the appropriate column for each raw score. Read down the column to the examinee's raw score, then read across the row to the extreme left or right column labeled Standardized Score to find the examinee's standardized score. Record each standard score on the summary page of the record form.

For the index scores on CVLT-II, the calculated raw score is used to derive the index score in the same manner as described for the trial scores. On CVLT3, the scaled scores for the designated trials are summed and used to derive the index scores. Index scores are provided for Trials 1–5, Delayed Recall (short-delay free recall, short-delay cued recall, long-delay free recall, and long-delay cued recall), and Total Recall (all recall trials). The index scores are derived using the full sample (all ages) because they are based on the sum of the age-corrected scaled scores. To obtain the index score, find the appropriate table for each raw score or sum of scaled scores. Read down the column to the examinee's raw score, then read across the row to the extreme left or right column labeled *T* Score/Standard Score to find the examinee's standardized index score. Record each standard score on the summary page of the record form.

DERIVING CVLT PROCESS SCORES

Many process scores can be derived on the CVLT; however, there are several process scores that are routinely used in clinical practice whereas others are used occasionally, with specific populations, or in research. This section details the steps required to derive those scores used commonly in clinical practice; to derive any additional process scores not described here you can refer to the appropriate manual or scoring software. Once you have derived the raw scores for the desired process scores, the standardized scores can be derived in the same manner described for the primary scores.

Rapid Reference 3.4

Process Scores Across Editions

Trial	CVLT-C score	CVLT-II score	CVLT3 score
Semantic Clustering	Observed Correct Semantic Clustering Expected Correct Semantic Clustering Ratio of Observed/Expected Semantic Clustering Global Semantic Clustering	Semantic Clustering (Observed) Semantic Clustering (Expected) Semantic Clustering (Chance Adjusted)	Trial 5 Semantic Clustering (Chance Adjusted) Trials 1–5 Semantic Clustering (Chance Adjusted)

Trial	CVLT-C score	CVLT-II score	CVLT3 score
Serial Clustering	Observed Correct Serial Clustering Expected Correct Serial Clustering Ratio of Observed/Expected Serial Clustering Global Serial Clustering	Serial Clustering Forward (Observed) Serial Clustering Forward (Expected) Serial Clustering Forward (Chance Adjusted)	Trials 1–5 Serial Clustering (Chance Adjusted)
Subjective Clustering	Not Available	Subjective Clustering Forward (Observed) Subjective Clustering Forward (Expected) Subjective Clustering Forward (Chance Adjusted)	Not Available
Learning Curve	Learning Slope	Total Learning Slope Learning Slope Trials 1–2 Learning Slope Trials 2–4 Learning Slope Trials 1–3 Learning Slope Trials 3–5	Trials 1–5 Learning Slope Analysis Trials 1–2 Learning Slope Analysis Trials 2–5 Learning Slope Analysis
Primacy, Middle, Recency	Percentage of Total Recall from: Primacy Region, Middle Region, and Recency Region	Percent Recall from Primacy Region, Middle Region, and Recency Region	Trials 1–5 Percent Recall Primacy Trials 1–5 Percent Recall Middle Trials 1–5 Percent Recall Recency
Recall Consistency	Percentage of Recall Consistency	Across-Trial Recall Consistency	Trials 1–5 Recall Consistency
Intrusions	Intrusions (Free- and Cued-Recall Total) Free-Recall Intrusions Cued-Recall Intrusions	Total Intrusions Free-Recall Intrusions Cued-Recall Intrusions Immediate Recall Intrusions Delayed-Recall Intrusions	Total Intrusions Trials 1–5 Intrusions Trials 1–4 Intrusions Delayed Recall Intrusions Free-Recall Intrusions Cued-Recall Intrusions Total Novel Intrusions Total Across/Within Trial Repeated Intrusions
Repetitions	Perseverations (Free- and Cued-Recall Total)	Total Repetitions	Total Repetitions Total Target Repetitions

Learning Characteristics

Evaluation of the strategies used to encode and recall words provides critical information on an examinee's learning and memory. The use of some strategies enhances performance while others may deter; more detailed information on the definition and interpretation of learning characteristic scores is provided in Chapter 4.

Semantic Clustering

Semantic clustering is the grouping of words together by semantic category during recall trials. For each edition, multiple scores are calculated for semantic clustering during the learning trials: Semantic Clustering (Observed), Semantic Clustering (Expected), and Semantic Clustering (Chance Adjusted). These scores are calculated for each trial and for Trials 1–5. The main score for interpretation is the Semantic Clustering (Chance Adjusted) score for Trials 1–5.

To calculate the Semantic Clustering (Observed) score, for each trial, indicate every time the examinee recalls a correct word from the same category as the immediately preceding correct word. You can use an arrow or numbering system on the record form to assist with scoring. In Figure 3.1, curved arrows are used to highlight semantic clusters. On the CVLT-C record form you can place a 1 next to each word in the Observed Semantic Cluster Score column. Sum the number of semantic clusters made within each learning trial to obtain the Semantic Clustering (Observed) raw score. Be sure not to include incorrect responses, including repetitions, in this raw score. In Figure 3.1, one semantic cluster was observed on Trial 1:

To calculate the Semantic Clustering (Expected) raw score, for each trial, use the following formula:

$$[(\text{number of correctly recalled words}) - 1]/[\text{number of categories} + 1].$$

If the examinee does not recall at least two words on a trial, semantic clustering cannot be calculated as it is impossible to cluster a single word. Be sure not to include incorrect responses, including repetitions, in this raw score. In Figure 3.1, the following values were obtained for Trial 1 and used in the formula:

$$[(6 - 1)/(4 + 1)] = 5/5 = 1$$

Calculate the Semantic Clustering (Chance Adjusted) for each trial by subtracting Semantic Clustering (Expected) from Semantic Clustering (Observed). To compute the raw score for Semantic Clustering (Chance Observed) for Trials 1–5, add the Semantic Clustering (Chance Adjusted) raw scores for each trial and divide by the number of trials in which the examinee recalled at least two words. In Figure 3.1, the following value was obtained for Trial 1.

$$[1 - 1] = 0$$

On CVLT-C, the calculation of the Expected Semantic Clustering score is different. For the expected score, you will need to determine the number of correctly recalled words from each category for each trial. For each category, multiply the number of correctly recalled words from that category by the number of correctly recalled words from the category minus 1 (i.e., correctly recalled words from category X [correctly recalled words from category – 1]). Divide this total by the number of words recalled (both correct and incorrect responses). Calculate this for each of the three categories and then sum the total for the five trials. In Figure 3.3, the Expected Semantic Clustering Score for Trial 1 is:

$$\text{Furniture: } (3 \times (3 - 1))/10 = 0.6$$

$$\text{Color: } (1 \times (1 - 1))/10 = 0$$

$$\text{Body Parts: } (2 \times (2 - 1))/10 = 0.2$$

$$\text{Trial 1 Total} = 0.6 + 0 + 0.2 = 0.8$$

Instead of a chance adjusted score, a Semantic Clustering Ratio Score is derived by dividing the sum of the observed semantic clustering trial raw score by the sum of the expected semantic clustering trial raw scores. In Figure 3.3, the observed semantic clustering scores for the trials are 2, 1, 2, 3, and 4 and the expected semantic clustering scores are 0.8, 0.77, 0.22, 2.0, and 2.4. Therefore the Semantic Clustering Ratio is 10/5.39 = 1.86.

Serial Clustering

Serial clustering is the grouping of words together on recall trials in the same order as they were presented during the learning trials. For each edition, multiple scores are calculated for semantic clustering during the learning trials; however, this chapter presents Serial Clustering (Observed), Serial Clustering (Expected), and Serial Clustering (Chance Adjusted). Note that these are labeled differently on each edition. These scores are calculated for each trial and for Trials 1–5. The main score for interpretation is the Serial Clustering (Chance Adjusted) score for Trials 1–5.

To calculate the Serial Clustering (Observed) score, for each trial, indicate every time the examinee recalls a correct word immediately after another correct word in the same order as presented on the list on the record form. You can use an arrow or numbering system on the record form to assist with scoring. In Figure 3.1, a vertical arrow highlight each serial cluster. On the CVLT-C, a table is provided in the record form to record the order in which words were recalled by the examinee for each trial. Sum the number of serial clusters made within each learning trial to obtain the Serial Clustering (Observed) raw score. Be sure not to include incorrect responses, including repetitions, in this raw score. In Figure 3.1, two semantic clusters were observed on Trial 1:

To calculate the Serial Clustering (Expected) raw score, for each trial, use the following formula:

$$[(\text{number of correctly recalled words}) - 1]/[\text{number of words in list}].$$

If the examinee does not recall at least two words on a trial, serial clustering cannot be calculated as it is impossible to cluster a single word. Be sure not to include incorrect

Fake List A	Trial 1		Trial 2		Trial 3		Trial 4		Trial 5	
sofa	*purple*	*C*	*brown*	*C*	*ankle*	*C*	*table*	*C*	*thumb*	*C*
purple	*chairs*	*C*	*purple*	*C*	*thumb*	*C*	*sofa*	*C*	*shoulder*	*C*
nose	*nightstand*	*C*	*chairs*	*C*	*nightstand*	*C*	*chairs*	*C*	*nose*	*C*
yellow	*thumb*	*C*	*yellow*	*C*	*chairs*	*C*	*ankle*	*C*	*bureau*	*C*
chair	*ankle*	*C*	*brown*	*R*	*yellow*	*C*	*brown*	*C*	*chairs*	*C*
arm	*sofa*	*C*	*bed*	*I*	*chair*	*R*	*orange*	*C*	*arm*	*C*
bureau	*purple*	*R*	*nightstand*	*C*	*bed*	*I*	*thumb*	*C*	*ear*	*R*
orange	*bed*	*I*	*ankle*	*C*	*P*		*nightstand*	*C*	*ankle*	*C*
thumb	~~*purple*~~		*pit*	*I*	*ear*	*I*	*sofa*	*R*	*brown*	*I*
nightstand	*P*		*P*		*bed*	*R/I*	*purple*	*C*	*purple*	*C*
ankle	*apple*	*I*					*P*		*P*	
brown	*couch*	*I*								
table										
blue										
shoulder										

Fake List B	Recall	
baseball	*grey*	*C*
grey	*pink*	*C*
pig	*silver*	*C*
pink	*ankle*	*I*
bowling	*monkey*	*C*
hamster	*ear*	*I*
hockey	*P*	
red	*pig*	*C*
monkey		
archery		
dog		
silver		
volleyball		
green		
goat		

Figure 3.3. Scoring sample trials 1–5 and interference trial for CVLT-C.

responses, including repetitions, in this raw score. In Figure 3.1, the following values were obtained for Trial 1 and used in the formula:

$$[(6-1)/16] = 5/16 = 0.3125$$

Calculate the Serial Clustering (Chance Adjusted) score for each trial by subtracting Serial Clustering (Expected) from Serial Clustering (Observed). To compute the raw score for Serial Clustering (Chance Observed) for Trials 1–5, add the Serial Clustering (Chance Adjusted) raw scores for each trial and divide by the number of trials in which the examinee recalled at least two words. In Figure 3.1, the following value was obtained for Trial 1.

$$[2 - 0.3125] = 1.6875 \textit{ or } 1.69$$

On CVLT-C, the calculation of the Expected Serial Clustering score is different. For the expected score, you will need to use the following formula:

$$[(1.35 \text{ X number of correctly recalled words on the trial})^{0.62} - 0.135]$$

Calculate this for each of the five trials and then sum the total for the five trials. For Trial 1 in Figure 3.3, $(1.35 \times 6^{0.62}) - 0.135 = 0.28$. Instead of a chance adjusted score, a Serial Clustering Ratio Score is derived by dividing the sum of the observed semantic clustering trial raw scores by the sum of the expected semantic clustering trial raw score. In Figure 3.3, the observed serial clustering scores for the trials are 0, 0, 1, 3, and 2 and the expected semantic clustering scores are 0.28, 0.28, 0.23, 0.39, and 0.39. Therefore the Serial Clustering Ratio is 6/1.57 = 3.82.

Learning Slope

The learning slope captures the average number of words an examinee is able to learn across trials. The first step in calculating the total learning slope is to create a sum table with the learning trial performance information in it. The table should include the trial number, the total correct for the trial, and some calculations required to complete the formula used to derive the score. See the following table:

Summary Table for T1–T5

Trial	Total correct	Trial squared	Trial X number correct
1	4	1	4
2	5	4	10
3	7	9	21
4	9	16	36
5	12	25	60
Sum of 1–5	37	55	131

You will use these values in the following formula to calculate the Learning Slope for Trials 1–5:

$$\frac{\sum xy - \left[\frac{(\sum x)(\sum y)}{n}\right]}{\sum x^2 - \left[\frac{(\sum x)^2}{n}\right]}$$

Where:

x = trial
y = total correct (per individual trial)
n = number of trials in slope
$\sum$ = sum

The same formula is used across all forms on CVLT-II and CVLT3 but the number of trials changes based on the form.

Primacy, Middle, Recency

Individuals recall words from the list differently if they are from the early (primacy), middle, or later (recency) part of the list. The percentage of words recalled from each part of the list can be calculated. To calculate these percentages, you must compare the recall of words by the examinee to the location of the words in the list presented. For the standard and alternate forms on CVLT-II and CVLT3, the first four words are the primacy region, the middle eight words are the middle region, and the last four words are the recency region. For the CVLT-II Short Form and CVLT3 Brief Form, the first three words are the primacy region, the middle three words are the middle region, and the last three words are the recency region. For CVLT-C, the first four words are the primacy region, the middle seven words are the middle region, and the last four words are the recency region.

Rapid Reference 3.5

Primacy, Middle, and Recency Differences Across Editions and Forms

Position	CVLT-C	CVLT-II standard/ alternate forms	CVLT-II brief form	CVLT3 standard/ alternate forms	CVLT3 short form
Primacy Region	First 4 words	First 4 words	First 3 words	First 4 words	First 3 words
Middle Region	Middle 7 words	Middle 8 words	Middle 3 words	Middle 8 words	Middle 3 words
Recency Region	Last 4 words	Last 4 words	Last 3 words	Last 4 words	Last 3 words

To calculate the percent recall from each region, classify each correctly recalled word by region. Then, for each trial, divide the words correctly recalled from each region by the total number of words correctly recalled for the trial and multiply by 100. To calculate the percentage of recall by region across the learning trials, sum the number of words correctly recalled across all trials and divide by the total number of words recalled correctly across all learning trials and multiply by 100. Note that only correct responses are considered in this calculation, do not use repetitions in the scores. In Figure 3.1, on Trial 1, two words of the six correct responses were from the primacy, two were from the middle, and two were from the recency region; therefore 33% of the correctly recalled words were from each region.

Recall Consistency

It is important to examine the consistency of recall across the learning trials. To calculate across trial recall consistency, sum the number of correctly recalled words that were also correctly recalled on the preceding trial. For example, if a target word is recalled on Trial 1 and then was also recalled in Trial 2, it would be counted in this total. Next, divide this sum by the total number of correctly recalled words across the first four learning trials (three for the Short/Brief form). Multiply the result of this calculation by 100 to obtain the percentage of words recalled consistently across the learning trials. In Figure 3.1, on Trial 2, three correct words were previously recalled during Trial 1; four words on Trial 3 were previously recalled on Trial 2. Note that thumb was not counted as it was not recalled on the trial immediately prior to Trial 3. On both Trials 4 and 5, five words were recalled on the previous trials. Therefore, the total number of consistently recalled words was 17. So recall consistency is (17/39) × 100% or 43.6%.

Recall Error Measures

Intrusions and Repetitions

To obtain the Total Intrusions scores, sum the intrusions recalled across all recall trials. Be sure to include all intrusions, regardless of type, across learning, interference, immediate recall, delayed recall, free-recall, and cued-recall trials. Total repetitions (perseverations) raw score is calculated in the same manner as total intrusions.

Raw scores for free-recall intrusions and cued-recall intrusions are also provided. Sum the number of intrusions from each learning, interference, short-delay and long-delay free-recall trial to obtain the free-recall intrusions raw score. Sum the number of intrusions made on the short-delay and long-delay cued-recall trials to obtain the cued-recall intrusions raw score. On CVLT3, sum the intrusions made during the learning trials to obtain the Trials 1–5 Intrusions raw score.

If you are hand scoring, transfer the raw scores for repetitions (perseverations) and intrusions to the summary page of the record form.

Novel and Across-/Within-Trial Repetition Errors

The CVLT3 introduced a new measure of consistency in relation to intrusions. Intrusions can be classified as novel or repeated across trials as well as the within-trial intrusions previously discussed. A novel across trial intrusion is an intrusion given by an examinee that has not been said on a previous trial. For this analysis, all recall trials are included so an intrusion given during long-delay free recall is not novel if it was recalled during the learning or immediate recall trials. It is important to note that intrusions from the interference trial are not counted as novel intrusions the first time they were given if they were recalled during the interference trial. Across-/Within-Trial repeated intrusions are intrusions that have been said previously, either within the trial or on a previous trial. For example, in Figure 3.1, on Trial 2 bed is an across/within trial intrusion because it was previously given in Trial 1. Sum the occurrence of novel intrusions and across-/within-trial repeated intrusions to obtain the raw scores for these errors, respectively.

Contrast Measures

Each edition of the CVLT evaluates the differences between standardized scores differently. These comparisons allow you to examine the differences in performance across trials to evaluate the impact of proactive and retroactive interference, as well as delay time on recall. The CVLT-C and CVLT-II calculate percent change values as well as simple difference scores (score 1–score 2) to evaluate change. Percentage of change utilizes the raw score differences while the simple difference method utilizes the standardized score differences. A common use is savings or retention scores. To calculate this score, divide the number of correctly recalled trials on short-delay free recall by the number of words correctly recalled on Trial 5. A similar calculation can be done for long-delay free recall.

The CVLT3 incorporates contrast scaled scores, which adjust one score based on the performance on another, related score. For example, the Long-Delay Free-Recall Correct vs. Trial 5 correct contrast scaled score describes the Long-Delay Free-Recall Correct score adjusted for performance on the Trial 5. The contrast scaled score represents the examinee's normative score in comparison to examinees with similar immediate memory ability. Contrast scores are derived from the entire standardization sample because they utilize age-adjusted scores. More information on the interpretation of contrast scaled scores is included in Chapter 4 of this book.

Rapid Reference 3.6

Contrast Measures Across Editions

Comparison	CVLT-C score	CVLT-II score	CVLT3 score
Immediate Attention (Interference Trial and Trial 1)	List B Free-Recall vs. List A Trial 1 Free-Recall Raw Percentage Change List B Free-Recall vs. List A Trial 1 Free-Recall Difference Score	List B Trial Versus List A Trial 1 Contrast Measure	List B Correct vs. Trial 1 Correct Contrast Scaled Score

Comparison	CVLT-C score	CVLT-II score	CVLT3 score
Short-Delay Savings (Short-Delay and Trial 5)	Short-Delay Free-Recall vs. List A Trial 5 Free-Recall Raw Percentage Change Short-Delay Free-Recall vs. List A Trial 5 Free-Recall Difference Score	Short-Delay Free-Recall and List A Trial 5 *z*-score Difference	Short-Delay Free-Recall Correct vs. Trial 5 Correct Contrast Scaled Score
Long-Delay Savings	Long-Delay Free-Recall vs. Short-Delay Free-Recall Raw Percentage Change Long-Delay Free-Recall vs. Short-Delay Free-Recall Difference Score	Long-Delay Free Recall and List A Trial 5 *z*-score Difference Long-Delay Free-Recall and Short-Delay Free-Recall *z*-score Difference	Long-Delay Free-Recall Correct vs. Trial 5 Correct Contrast Scaled Score Long-Delay Free-Recall Correct vs. Short-Delay Free-Recall Correct Contrast Scaled Score
Recognition vs. Recall (Recognition Discriminability and Long-Delay Recall)	Recognition Discriminability vs. Long-Delay Free-Recall Raw Percentage Change Recognition Discriminability vs. Long-Delay Free-Recall Difference Score	Total Recognition Discriminability (*d'*) and Long-Delay Free-Recall *z*-score Difference	Long-Delay Free-Recall Correct vs. Recognition Discriminability (*d'*) Contrast Scaled Score Long-Delay Free-Recall Discriminability vs. Recognition Discriminability (*d'*) Contrast Scaled Score

Forced-Choice Recognition Measures (CVLT-II and CVLT3)

Forced-Choice is the only optional trial on the CVLT. The raw score on this trial is the number of correct responses (Hits) on the items. Note that an *I don't know* or no response is counted and scored as an error/incorrect response. This raw score can be compared to the percentage of individuals in the standardization sample who obtained a similar score.

Additional Scores

Many other process scores can be derived on the CVLT editions; however, most scores require the scoring programs to derive and are not specifically detailed in the hand scoring instructions. Refer to the appropriate manual or scoring software for more information on how to obtain these scores. It is important to note that process scores are not consistent across all the CVLT editions and that more scores may be described in the research literature.

Computer Scoring Procedures

All three editions of the CVLT can be administered on Q-interactive. Independent scoring assistants are available for CVLT-C and CVLT-II but the software is old and not compatible with newer software systems. The CVLT3 can be scored via the Q-global system. To obtain all the scores in these systems, you will need to enter all verbatim words said by the examinee and then classify the intrusions. Correct responses can be selected within each of the programs and do not require further classification as repetitions are automatically classified for words from the word lists. The scoring programs provide all the raw and standardized scores possible for the trials entered. The CVLT3 also provides education and sex-adjusted scores through Q-global. The scoring program increases accuracy of scoring and decreases the overall scoring time for CVLT. Depending upon the edition, the related scoring assistant produces a score report that includes the following:

- Raw and Standardized Score Table for the Primary Measures
- Summary table for process scores, both overall and by trial and subgroupings of trials
- Summary of the contrast measures, including both percentage of change and difference scores or contrast scaled scores, if appropriate
- Graphical depictions of performance on the learning trials, including correct responses, repetitions, intrusions, and clustering
- Graphical depictions of performance on the short-delay and long-delay recall trials, including correct responses, repetitions, intrusions, and clustering
- Summary table of all responses across all trials and the classifications for each responses

TEST YOURSELF

1. What do you do when an examinee refuses to answer a question on Yes/No recognition?

(a) Wait until the examinee responds, continue to prompt for them to guess

(b) Move onto the next item and code the response as a *No*

(c) Move onto the next item but no total score is calculated for the trial

(d) Stop administration of the trial as no scores can be calculated

2. **What do you do when an examinee refuses to answer a question on Forced-Choice Recognition?**
   (a) Move onto the next item but no total score is calculated for the trial
   (b) Stop administration of the trial as no scores can be calculated
   (c) Wait until the examinee responds, continue to prompt for them to guess
   (d) Move onto the next item and code the response as an incorrect response
3. **The most accurate and efficient approach to scoring is to use scoring software.**
   True or False
4. **Scores are derived in the same manner across all editions of CVLT.**
   True or False

Use the following responses for Trials 1–5 to answer questions 5–11.

Fake list A	Trial 1		Trial 2		Trial 3		Trial 4		Trial 5	
sofa	*sofa*		*sofa*		*sofa*		*sofa*		*sofa*	
purple	*purple*		*purple*		*purple*		*chair*		*chair*	
nose	*nose*		*nose*		*baseball*		*ankle*		*bureau*	
baseball	*ankle*		*yellow*		*hockey*		*bureau*		*hockey*	
yellow	*chin*		*orange*		*chair*		*yellow*		*archery*	
chair	*hockey*		*P*		*ankle*		*blue*		*orange*	
archery	*P*		*brown*		*chin*		*arm*		*brown*	
arm	*nose*		*orange*		*brown*		*nose*		*nose*	
bureau			*couch*		*orange*		*ankle*		*bowling*	
hockey					*nose*		*hockey*		*chair*	
orange					*P*		*blue*		*sofa*	
thumb					*bowling*		*P*		*P*	
bowling					*pig*		*ankle*		*thumb*	
nightstand							*pig*		*nose*	
ankle							*couch*		*chairs*	
brown										

5. **For Trial 1, what are the correct classifications for the responses?**
   (a) Correct, Correct, Correct, Correct, Intrusion, Correct, Repetition
   (b) Correct, Correct, Correct, Intrusion, Repetition, Correct, Correct
   (c) Correct, Correct, Intrusion, Correct, Repetition, Intrusion, Correct
   (d) Correct, Correct, Correct, Correct, Repetition, Correct, Repetition

6. For Trial 4, what are the correct classifications for the responses?
   (a) Correct, Correct, Intrusion, Correct, Repetition, Correct, Correct, Intrusion, Repetition, Repetition, Intrusion, Repetition, Repetition
   (b) Correct, Correct, Correct, Correct, Correct, Repetition, Intrusion, Correct, Correct, Intrusion, Intrusion, Repetition, Repetition
   (c) Correct, Correct, Correct, Correct, Correct, Intrusion, Correct, Correct, Repetition, Correct, Repetition/Intrusion, Intrusion
   (d) Correct, Correct, Correct, Correct, Correct, Intrusion, Correct, Correct, Correct, Correct, Repetition/Intrusion, Repetition, Intrusion

7. Which of the following is a category intrusion on Trial 3?
   (a) Nose
   (b) Chin
   (c) Pig
   (d) None of the above

8. What is the raw score for total repetitions on Trial 5?
   (a) 1
   (b) 2
   (c) 3
   (d) 4

9. What are the total correct raw scores for Trials 1–5?
   (a) 5, 6, 10, 7, 10
   (b) 7, 8, 12, 13, 14
   (c) 5, 8, 10, 7, 14
   (d) 7, 6, 12, 13, 10

10. Which of the following is an example of a subordinate/synonym intrusion on Trial 2?
   (a) Pig
   (b) Blue
   (c) Couch
   (d) None of the above

11. Which of the following is an example of semantic clustering?
   (a) Trial 1 ankle—chin
   (b) Trial 3 orange—nose
   (c) Trial 5 thumb—nose
   (d) Trial 4 sofa—chair

Use the following responses for Trials 1–5 for question 12.

Furniture		**Colors**		**Body parts**		**Sports**	
chair	C	*purple*	C	*thumb*	C	*baseball*	C
bed	I	*yellow*	C	*ankle*	C	*soccer*	I
sofa	C	*red*	I	*orange*	C*	*P*	
P		*P*		*nose*	C		
				P			

*Note that this would be an intrusion on CVLT-II but is a correct response on CVLT3.

12. **What is the cued-recall trial total correct for the CVLT-II and CVLT3, respectively?**
    (a) 9, 10
    (b) 10, 9
    (c) 12, 9
    (d) 9, 12

Answers: 1. b, 2. d, 3. True, 4. False, 5. a, 6. c, 7. b, 8. b; 9. a, 10. c, 11. d, 12. a

Four

INTERPRETATION OF THE CVLT

Despite its brevity, the California Verbal Learning Test (CVLT) provides robust information about multiple aspects of learning and memory. Memory is more than an individual's ability to recall information; successful learning and memory function require several aspects of cognitive functioning working together to facilitate encoding, retrieval, and recognition. At the most basic level, the CVLT is a test of verbal episodic memory. However, with careful consideration and practice interpreting the CVLT, you can examine other important aspects of an individual's memory, including strategies used to learn and recall information, recency and primacy effects, proactive and retroactive interference, learning slope, and recall consistency. If there is a breakdown in an individual's memory performance, the CVLT allows examination of which aspect of the learning or recall process is failing. In clinical practice, this information can provide valuable insight into which cognitive functions and processes may be implicated in memory deficits and therefore lead to better diagnoses and interventions.

Interpretation of the CVLT can feel overwhelming at times. There are over 60 different scores available for the CVLT3 (CVLT-C and CVLT-II have a similar number of scores to consider). For someone new to the CVLT, it can be difficult to know where to focus and how to integrate findings into a psychological or neuropsychological report. In practice, however, it is unlikely that you would include all possible scores in a report. In most cases, you will instead focus on how well an examinee acquired or learned the list of words, how well they retained those words, and how well they recalled the words. Only in certain situations would a clinical report make mention of additional detailed aspects of the learning approach. Chapter 7 of this manual provides clinical examples of how specific patient populations perform on the CVLT and how careful

CAUTION 4.1

The CVLT is not a stand-alone test for diagnosing specific conditions such as dementia. Interpretation of the CVLT is done in conjunction with a comprehensive cognitive evaluation and in the context of other clinically relevant information gathered during assessment (e.g., educational history, developmental history, medical history, performance on attention and executive function tests, psychiatric history and current level of distress, sleep impairment, chronic pain, effort or test engagement, and English language fluency).

interpretation of the CVLT can help the clinician narrow in on a differential diagnosis. This chapter covers the basic approach to the interpretation of the CVLT, beginning with a few basic principles of interpretation that are applicable to all versions of the CVLT. This is followed by a simple approach to understanding the primary scores capturing overall learning and memory capacity. Finally, interpretation of the scores related to the processes involved in learning and recall is addressed. For the purposes of this chapter, note that the CVLT-C, CVLT-II, and CVLT3 all have similar structures and designs. As such, interpretation can be generalized across all CVLT versions. Specific considerations are mentioned for each version where appropriate.

FACTORS THAT AFFECT INTERPRETATION

Scores obtained on any assessment reflect the examinee's ability as well as measurement error. Factors that influence test performance may be inherent to the test and will be called out when appropriate but individual factors can also influence performance. Multiple factors influence verbal memory and should be considered in the interpretation of the CVLT. The following list provides information on factors known to influence performance on verbal memory measures and guidance on how to administer or interpret CVLT in order to minimize their influence on interpretation.

1. Expressive and receptive verbal abilities: The CVLT requires an examinee to verbally respond during recall trials. In the case of severe language disorders, aphasia or dysarthria, the CVLT may not be appropriate and results may underestimate an individual's true memory ability. For less severe language difficulties, you must consider the impact of the language difficulties in interpreting results and may need to modify procedures to accommodate deficits. All modifications should be noted in the report.
2. English language proficiency: The CVLT was normed on individuals fluent in English. Although English fluency is required, you should establish whether the individual you are testing is a native English speaker or whether English was acquired later in life. This information should be documented in a clinical report and considered in the interpretation of the findings.
3. Acute changes in mental status: In certain clinical situations, including delirium and acute psychosis, the individual you are testing may not have the capacity to perform the evaluation and any assessment would certainly misrepresent his or her true abilities. The CVLT is not a measure of mental status, but an individual's mental status could have an impact on performance. As such, mental status should be assessed in some way prior to administration of the CVLT.
4. Hearing function: Reduced hearing abilities can negatively influence test performance. This can be quite subtle (e.g., mild misperception of a word, such as hearing "Trunk" instead of "Truck") or profound (e.g., missing several items due to failed hearing). Deficits in hearing should be discussed in the clinical interview and

accommodation should be made during testing. Accommodations might include hearing aids or amplifiers. It can be helpful to have spare headphone sound amplifiers in case the need should arise. If such hearing aids or amplifiers are insufficient to correct hearing, the CVLT should not be used as a measure of memory. Sometimes people simply have mildly attenuated hearing that affects perception in subtler ways. If misperceptions are suspected due to poor hearing, this should be considered in the clinical interpretation of the findings.

5. Demographic factors, including age, education, sex, and race or ethnicity: Demographic factors are important in the clinical interpretation of testing data but such variables are often proxies of other underlying factors that are more difficult to measure objectively. For instance, education level does not capture quality of education, opportunities within the school, achievement within the classroom, or educational standards, factors that differ widely regionally and even within a school. Therefore, whereas some specific demographic variables (e.g., age) directly affect CVLT performance, others are proxies for numerous underlying variables (e.g., education, race/ethnicity).
   a. Age is perhaps the most obvious demographic factor affecting CVLT performance. In children, teens tend to recall more words, engage in more sophisticated learning strategies, and retain more words over time than their younger counterparts. In adults (CVLT-II and CVLT3), age is negatively correlated with performance; age accounts for 25.9% of the variance in CVLT-II performance (Lezak, Howieson, Bigler, & Tranel, 2012). As age increases, adults demonstrate improved performance until middle age and then after middle age, they recall fewer target words and display more false positives on recognition (Huh, Kramer, Gazzaley, & Delis, 2006). Be sure to look at age-correct standard scores instead of relying on raw scores to minimize the influence of age on interpretation.
   b. Educational attainment or educational quality: Differences in educational background influence an examinee's experience with English, vocabulary, semantic categorization, and use of memory strategies. Education accounts for only 4.5% of the variance in CVLT-II performance (Lezak et al., 2012), but it should still be considered when interpreting test performance.
   c. Sex: Women recall an average of five more words across Trials 1–5 and demonstrate stronger semantic clustering than men (CVLT-II; Lezak et al., 2012). Differences between girls and boys have also been found on the CVLT-C. Girls recalled more items than boys on all learning trials and on the delay recall trial, and outperformed boys on recognition trials. Additionally, boys made more false-positive errors and more intrusions than girls. Lastly, girls were more likely to use semantic clustering and displayed stronger recall of primacy and middle regions of the list compared to boys (Kramer, Delis, Kaplan, O'Donnell, & Prifitera, 1997).
   d. Race/ethnicity: Race has very little to do with performance, accounting for only 0.3% of the variance in CVLT-II scores (Lezak et al., 2012).

UNDERSTANDING SCORES FROM THE CVLT

DON'T FORGET 4.1

Remember this basic psychometric principle: An individual's true score is his or her observed score plus measurement error or True Score = Observed Score + Error. Always consider sources of error when interpreting scores.

A comprehensive review of test statistics and psychometrics is beyond the scope of this chapter. However, a brief review of the scores included in the CVLT will aid you in understanding the interpretive report. Each version of the CVLT provides different types of standardized scores. These include *z*-scores, standard scores, scaled scores, and *T* scores. The CVLT-II and CVLT3 utilize the same word lists, but one important change to the CVLT3 was the inclusion of scaled scores instead of *z*-scores. Therefore, be aware of the scores you are looking at in the printed score report to avoid misinterpretation.

Standardized scores normalize data to a standard metric, based on the distribution of the normal curve. Although the mean and standard deviation (SD) for any type of standardized score may vary, the percentage of the sample falling within specific distances (standard deviations) from the mean remains the same. All standardized scores are centered around a mean with a known standard deviation. The *z*-score, for example, is scaled so that the mean is 0 and the standard deviation is 1 point in either direction on the normal curve. A negative *z*-score (e.g., −1.0) indicates that the associated raw score was one standard deviation below the mean score. A positive *z*-score (e.g., 1.0) indicates that the associated raw score was one standard deviation above the mean score. For the CVLT-C and CVLT-II, the available range of *z*-scores is −5 to +5 (five standard deviations below and above the mean), and scores are reported in 0.5 point increments. For the learning and recall trials, a higher *z*-score indicates better performance. However, for the recency-recall index and the error scores (discussed below), higher *z*-scores suggest worse performance. Several of the CVLT raw scores provide a corresponding *z*-score, so it is critical to have a foundational understanding of *z*-scores and their interpretation.

CAUTION 4.2

For learning and recall trials, a higher *z*-score indicates better performance. However, for the recency-recall index and the error scores, higher *z*-scores suggest worse performance (applicable to CVLT-C and CVLT-II). On CVLT3, higher scores are always associated with better performance.

The CVLT3 replaced *z*-scores with scaled scores. Scaled scores use a mean of 10 and a standard deviation of 3. The possible range for scaled scores on the CVLT3 is 1–19, reflecting 3 standard deviations in either direction of a mean of 10. On CVLT3, higher scores always reflect better performance. All versions of the CVLT use a *T* score for at least some scores. A *T* score is scaled to have a mean of 50 and a standard deviation of 10. For example, a *T* score of 40 would be 1 standard deviation below the standardization sample mean. Another addition to the CVLT3 was the inclusion of standard scores, which

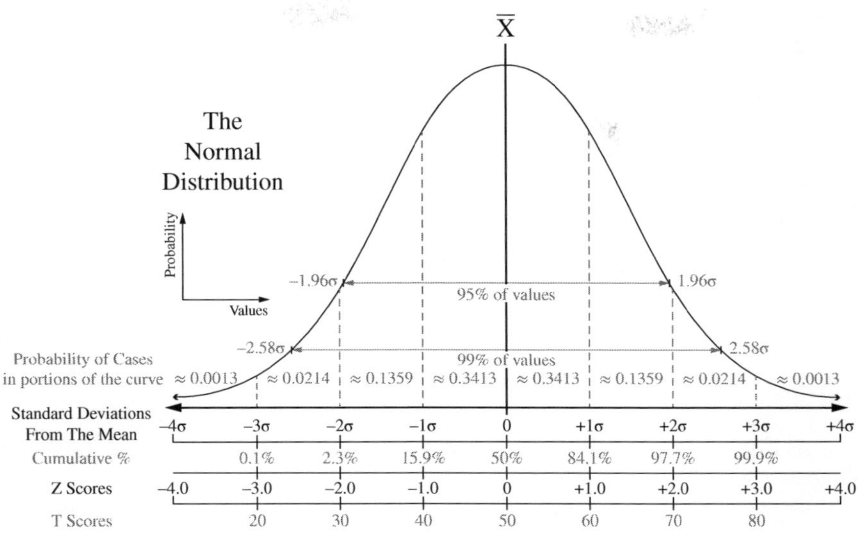

Figure 4.1. CVLT standardized scores on the normal curve.

provide indices of overall learning and memory. These standard scores have a mean of 100 and a standard deviation of 15 (range of 40–160 reflecting 4 standard deviations in either direction from the mean).

For a novice clinician, the various forms of standardized scores can be confusing, especially in scenarios of repeated assessments across time in which an examinee may be given different versions of the CVLT. However, it is important to keep in mind that all standardized scores can be converted and thus compared to any other standardized score. For example, a standard deviation change is interpreted the same way, regardless of which metric is used (*z* versus *T* versus scaled score). Thus, a *z*-score of +1 is the same as a *T* score of 60, which is the same as a scaled score of 13 and a standard score of 115. All these scores are 1 standard deviation above the mean. Figure 4.1 illustrates the position of the various scores on the normal curve distribution.

Now that you have considered clinical variables that can impact the interpretation of scores and understand standardized scores, it is time to dive into the interpretation of the scores of the CVLT.

INTERPRETATION OF CVLT PRIMARY SCORES

Multiple scores are available for the interpretation of the CVLT. Which scores you utilize is determined by the needs of the individual being assessed and the referral questions. Each aspect of the test is enumerated and detailed next. However, for simplicity, we recommend beginning with the primary scores and then examining more detailed process scores as needed. This is akin to taking a macro-level view before beginning a deeper dive into finer details of an examinee's performance.

We suggest beginning interpretation by examining the following scores:

1. Trial 1 Total Correct
2. Trials 1–5 Total Correct (Short Form includes Trials 1–4)
3. Interference Trial: List B (no interference trial on Short Form)
4. Short-Delay Recall (Free Recall and Cued Recall; no Short-Delay Cued Recall on Short/Brief Form)
5. Long-Delay Recall (Free Recall and Cued Recall)
6. Yes/No Recognition

When you interpret these primary scores first, you will have a basic sense of how well the examinee learned and retained information.

Trial 1 Total Correct

Trial 1 of List A is the first presentation of the word list so the examinee's recall provides an assessment of his or her verbal attention span. Whereas the focus of t he CVLT is on learning and retention of material, Trial 1 is a reflection of the examinee's immediate attention capacity. The average performance of the normative reference populations for the CVLT-C, CVLT-II, and CVLT3 is similar to the number 7+ or −2 often referenced in attention span tests, such as digit span. The Trial 1 correct score is highly correlated to other auditory working memory tests, such as Digit Span from the Wechsler Adult Intelligence Scale (WAIS)-III (Delis, Cullum, Butters, Cairns, & Prifitera, 1988; Delis, Freeland, Kramer, & Kaplan, 1988; The Psychological Corporation, 1997).

Rapid Reference 4.1

- CVLT-C Trial 1 mean score ranges from 5 to 7 in young children and teenagers, respectively.
- CVLT-II Trial 1 has a mean of 6.62 among those ages 16–60.
- CVLT3 Trial 1 has a mean of 6.5 among those ages 16–60.

An individual's score on Trial 1 of List A can provide clinically meaningful information when considered in the context of other learning trials, total learning, and other verbal working memory measures. When an individual's score is very low on Trial 1, but subsequently normal on Trials 2–5 and Trials 1–5 Total, this can signify poor attention abilities. Additionally, the initial trial could be overwhelming to the examinee. Individuals with depression or anxiety may feel frustrated by the length of the first trial but improve on re-presentation of the list. As an example, a 35-year-old female with a history of severe anxiety and depression was referred for a comprehensive evaluation. Her learning trial total raw scores for the CVLT3 were 3, 8, 10, 15, and 16 for a total of 52, which is an average score for Trials 1–5 Total score in this individual's age range. However, a total raw score of 3 on Trial 1 is low for her age and well below her ability to recall eight digits forward on digit span. Given that her attention capacity was considered normal on a digit span task, her initial poor performance on Trial 1 may have been due to anxiety. Digit span is less vulnerable to anxiety because most measures begin with only two numbers and repeating two digits and gradually increasing one digit at a time is less stressful than beginning with 15–16 items right from the first trial. In Chapter 6, we provide another example of how anxiety may influence the first trial while the remaining learning trials are considered normal.

Alternatively, some individuals may have average initial recall on Trial 1 of List A, but then show a flat learning curve and reduced overall learning across learning trials. An incremental improvement with each trial is typically expected unless you are testing someone with excellent memory who obtains the maximum raw score on each trial. An inability to incrementally gain more words on subsequent trials can be abnormal. It is helpful to compare Trial 1 to the Interference Trial and to other working memory tests, such as digit span. In certain situations, an examinee may have normal working memory and similar working memory scores across tests but show overall poor learning. For example, those with medial temporal abnormalities (e.g., Alzheimer's disease) may demonstrate an average score for Trial 1, average performance on List B, and average Digit Span performance, but exhibit a flat learning curve since medial temporal damage may preclude them from being able to surpass their working memory capacity and achieve incremental learning across trials.

When comparing Digit Span, or similar working memory tests, to Trial 1, it is important to recognize differing patient experiences with the test. As noted briefly previously, a digit span task typically starts with a short string of numbers, which is not very taxing to working memory. Comparatively, a long list of words is considered a supraspan (the number of words exceeds typical working memory capacity). For those with depression or anxiety, starting with a long list of words can be overwhelming, and they may not recall much on Trial 1. Conversely, individuals with a problem with auditory processing or auditory sequencing may perform better on Trial 1 than they do on a digit span task. This is thought to occur because digit span requires individuals to repeat a string of numbers in the correct order whereas the CVLT words can be repeated in any order. For those who struggle to maintain focus and concentration (e.g., children with attention deficit/hyperactivity disorder (ADHD) or other developmental disorders), poor performance on Trial 1 may be associated with behaviors of poor focus in the classroom or other settings that require working memory.

Rapid Reference 4.2

Expectations for Trial 1

Note that CVLT Short Form does not have a List B. List A versus List B is a distinguishing feature only of standard and alternate forms. Also, the short form has only four learning trials.

(continued)

What is expected performance on Trial 1 of List A?

1. Overall recall capacity should be similar to performance on other working memory tests.
2. Those with normal working memory but poor learning may display a flat learning curve and/or overall poor learning.
3. A low score on Trial 1 Total Correct could be related to anxiety or other mood factors when other remaining learning trials or total learning are normal. Otherwise, a pathologically low initial recall may be related to true deficits in working memory. You should examine other clinically relevant behaviors or symptoms to confirm whether such factors are present and could affect testing.

Trials 1–5 Total Correct

After five learning trials, the CVLT provides robust data on the immediate free-recall abilities of the examinee. The standardized score for the total learning across all learning trials provides a global measure of immediate free recall of auditory information. When an examinee's standardized score is average or higher, learning abilities may be intact. However, even an average score on Trials 1–5 Total Correct, valuable information can be obtained by examining the learning characteristics. More detailed information on learning characteristics is provided in the next section, but for now, consider the following example. Two individuals obtain a Trials 1–5 Total Correct score in the average range, with a raw score of 40. Patient A obtained the following trial raw totals: 3, 5, 7, 10, and 15 for a total of 40. Patient B obtained the following trial raw totals: 7, 8, 8, 9, and 8 for a total of 40. Both patients obtained the same Trials 1–5 Total Correct standardized score; however, learning was very different across the two patients. Note that it is entirely possible that these two score patterns could be obtained by the same individual across two test sessions. Assume the examinee obtained the first set of scores and then the second set at a follow-up 1 year later. Would learning be considered better at time one or time two? Would differences be clinically meaningful? Next, consider the scenario in which an individual obtains a low Trials 1–5 Total Correct score. For example, performance across the learning trials yields a scaled score of 4 (two standard deviations below the mean). In this case, you could reasonably conclude that immediate memory or learning abilities are below expectation. However, further exploration of the examinee's learning style can provide valuable insight into clinical considerations.

Interference Trial: List B (Standard and Alternate Forms Only)

Immediately following the administration of the learning trials, an interference trial consisting of a new list of words is administered. List B is an immediate recall trial. There are still latent semantic categorizations in the list, with some categories shared between List A and B (e.g., "fruits") and some nonshared categories (e.g., "furniture" items on List B but not List A). Having shared and unshared semantic categories allows for examination of proactive interference between List A and List B.

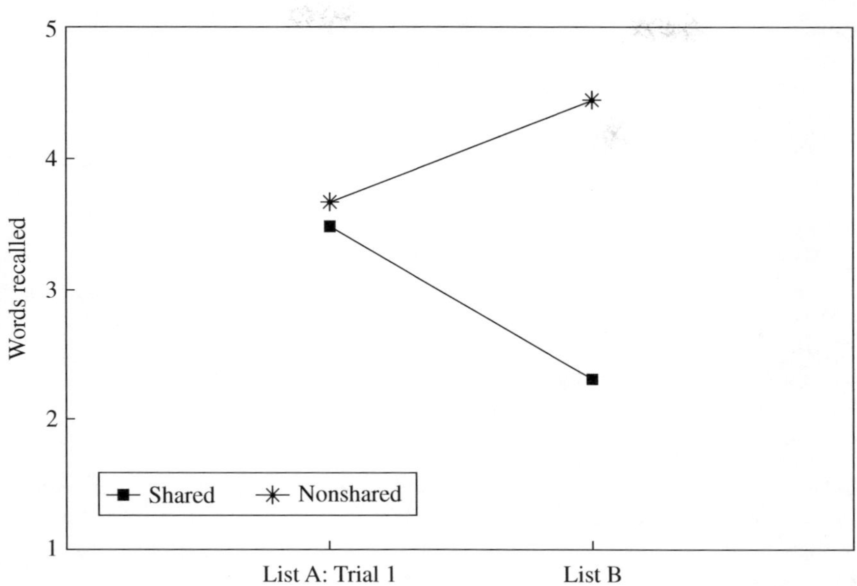

Figure 4.2. Proactive interference displayed as mean recall of shared and unshared items for CVLT (Kramer & Delis, 1991).

Proactive interference occurs when previously learned information interferes with the efficiency of acquiring new information. At least some degree of proactive interference is considered normal. Kramer and Delis (1991) examined proactive interference in 270 nonclinical individuals. Examinees recalled an equivalent number of words from shared and nonshared categories on Trial 1. However, when List B was introduced, the number of nonshared category words recalled increased by 21% while the number of shared-category words recalled decreased by 33% (See Figure 4.2).

As with Trial 1, recalling a list for the first time is a measure of attention and auditory working memory. However, List B is unique because it requires auditory working memory and inhibition of interference from hearing List A multiple times. Therefore, it is normal to recall one or two fewer items on List B than what was initially recalled on Trial 1 of List A. It would be unusual to have a substantially lower score on List B than Trial 1. Contrast scores and savings scores, which are described later in this chapter, can provide information about the consistency of recall ability between Trial 1 and List B.

In the CVLT, proactive interference is indicated by comparing performance on Trial 1 and List B. List B vs. Trial 1 is presented as the percent of the difference in raw scores on these trials. For example, if Trial 1 raw score is 4 and List B raw score is 3, the percentage retained would be listed in the report as −25%, with a *z*-score of 0 (58-year-old male examinee). However, if Trial 1 is a raw score of 7 and List B is a raw score of 9, the percentage would be listed in the report as a +28.6%, with a *z*-score of 0.5 (44-year-old female examinee). Both of these differences are within the average range. Retention or savings scores are available only for CVLT-II and CVLT-C.

Proactive interference can manifest in several ways on the CVLT:

1. Immediate recall of List B may be lower than recall of Trial 1 because of interference from the learning of List A. Immediate learning trials interfere with learning and recall of List B.
2. Recall of words from the shared categories between the two lists could result in a lower score on List B due to the semantic similarity between the lists. This implies that the semantic category "sticks" and these words are more likely to be recalled. Thus, there may be more intrusions from shared categories with List A.
3. The examinee may display cross-trial intrusions in which they recall items from List A only during recall for List B.

Clinical Considerations

Differences between Trial 1 and List B may arise from both cognitive and noncognitive factors. For instance, significant variability in learning and recall across trials is observed in the presence of attentional deficits or nonneurological factors, such as chronic pain or anxiety. It is important to note that proactive interference is not necessarily expected in all examinees. For instance, in conditions affecting medial temporal lobe functioning, such as Alzheimer's disease, examinees may not recall enough of List A to interfere substantially with List B recall.

Short-Delay Recall

Short-Delay Free Recall

Immediately after the presentation and free recall of List B, the examinee is asked to recall words from List A again. (Note the Short Form does not have a List B but rather a 30-s distractor task requiring the examinee to count backward from 100.) This short-delay recall is done without prior warning and without hearing the list again. Short-delay free recall is a direct measure of retention of verbal information following a short passage of time. In other words, the CVLT recall trials assess the preservation of verbal memory. Scores from this short-delay free recall can be considered in a few ways. First, recall of List A at this point could be lower than the total recall of Trial 5 from the learning trials because of retroactive interference. Retroactive interference occurs when new information interferes with recall of previously learned information. Specifically,

DON'T FORGET 4.2

- Proactive Interference: Previously learned information affects recall of new information (e.g., List A interferes with List B).
- Retroactive Interference: Newly learned information interferes with recall of previous information (e.g., List B interferes with List A, such as in short-delay free recall).

having just attempted to recall List B, this new information interferes with recall of List A. As such, it is common to have a slightly lower raw score for items of List A recalled at the short-delay free-recall trial than on Trial 5. Short-delay free recall could also be reduced simply because of the delay of time (i.e., recall of 15 or 16 words immediately after hearing them could be different than recall after 2–3 min).

Another consideration in the interpretation of short-delay free recall is the difference between the raw score and the percentage of retained information from the learning trials. For instance, if Trial 5 recall was lower than expected for a healthy adult, say seven words, and the same seven words are recalled at the short-delay free-recall trial, the percentage of retention (also called savings) is 100%. This is normal retention, despite the low learning score. However, if the examinee recalls nearly all the words, with a score of 15 on Trial 5 of List A, but then recalls only seven items on the short-delay free-recall trial, this is a retention of only 47%, which is quite low for a healthy person. Therefore, it is prudent to examine the amount of information recalled (i.e., the total recall score) as well as the retention of information previously recalled.

Clinical Considerations

Distinct memory profiles are observable when examining the level of recall and percentage of retention.

Profile 1: This profile occurs when the level of recall is high (i.e., good learning and recall) and the percentage of retention is high (i.e., strong savings). This pattern is often observed in healthy children and adults and indicates good learning and memory.

Profile 2: This profile occurs when the level of recall is low (i.e., low learning and low recall) but the percentage of retention is high (i.e., strong savings). This pattern is often observed in psychiatric disorders and among individuals with subcortical processes, such as Huntington's disease or Parkinson's disease, and indicates poor learning but good retention of information learned.

Profile 3: This profile occurs when the level of recall is low (i.e., impaired learning) and the percent retention is also low (i.e., low savings). This pattern indicates poor learning; retention may be low simply because of poor learning or because of rapid decay of the low amount of information recalled in learning trials.

Profile 4: This profile occurs when retention is substantially lower than expected based on relatively intact learning as demonstrated by low short-delay free recall and low percentage of retention (i.e., higher learning and lower retention). This can occur in conditions having an impact on medial temporal functioning, such as Alzheimer's disease, left-temporal epilepsy, Korsakoff's syndrome, or hippocampal sclerosis, and indicates poor recall and retention. This pattern is potentially related to poor encoding or consolidation to long-term memory.

Short-Delay Cued Recall

Immediately following the short-delay free-recall trial, the examinee is asked to recall words from List A based on a semantic cue (i.e., "tell me all the words from the first list that are animals"). This allows you to examine whether cues help the examinee recall information. In individuals with intact memory abilities, a cue facilitates recall, such that more words are recalled with cueing than are freely recalled. It also provides a potential strategy to the examinee for recalling words.

DON'T FORGET 4.3

- Semantic clustering occurs when the examinee groups words together that are of the same category (e.g., fruits).
- Serial clustering occurs when the examinee attempts to recall the words in the same order provided by the examiner, regardless of semantic groupings.

One scenario involves recalling a substantially higher number of words under the cued-recall condition compared to the free-recall condition. This pattern suggests that the examinee benefited from semantic cues and that more words were encoded into memory than the examinee could freely recall. In other words, the examinee displayed retrieval deficits. This can occur for a number of reasons. Improvement with semantic cueing can be seen among examinees who failed to use semantic clustering or who were more prone to use serial clustering during the learning trials. Semantic clustering is positively correlated with executive skills and individuals using serial clustering often display difficulties in the executive initiation of encoding and recall during the learning trials (see process score section for more information on learning characteristics). Individuals who did not previously engage in semantic clustering tend to have a higher performance under cued conditions relative to free recall.

Individuals who used semantic clustering during the learning trials may not have any new incremental benefit from hearing the cues because they were already using this clustering method. In this case, cued-recall performance is likely to be similar to the free-recall performance. For some individuals, semantic clustering can have a detrimental effect, with a lower performance on cued recall relative to free recall. For instance, children with verbal learning deficits may have general language processing difficulties, which can result in more effortful recall when restrained to a single semantic grouping. This was observed by Shear, Tallal, and Delis (1992), who demonstrated that such children obtained lower scores on cued recall than free recall. Similarly, children with Down syndrome may demonstrate reduced cued recall relative to free recall, ostensibly due to reduced general verbal skills (Bellugi, Bihrle, Neville, Doherty, & Jernigan, 1992).

With any cued-recall condition, another important factor to consider in interpretation is the presence of intrusions. An intrusion occurs when an examinee responds with a word that was not on List A. When these errors are novel words, not words from List B, they are often referred to as confabulatory errors. It can be helpful to examine the number of intrusions provided in free recall compared to cued recall. When there are more intrusions on cued recall, the semantic prompt by the examiner may have induced confabulation. There are a few clinical conditions that are vulnerable to confabulation. For instance, individuals with Korsakoff's syndrome often confabulate on free recall and cued recall. Those with Alzheimer's disease (AD) may display very poor recall with an amnestic pattern but will often engage in free association when given a semantic prompt. Other patient groups who may confabulate include those with schizophrenia, fetal alcohol spectrum disorders, Down syndrome, Williams syndrome, traumatic brain injury, and stroke.

CAUTION 4.3

Do not confuse confabulation with poor effort or malingering. Confabulation is a symptom observed in clinical populations that is not intended to mislead the examiner. Typically there is not a secondary gain associated with confabulation. Malingering is the intentional lowering of performance to feign or exaggerate deficits and typically involves secondary gain.

There are a few different clinical considerations in the interpretation of scores when comparing free-recall versus cued-recall conditions. First, keep in mind that there are developmental differences in children's free recall and cued recall on the CVLT-C. Young children are less proficient with using retrieval than their preadolescent and teenage counterparts (Kramer et al., 1997). In healthy groups, younger children display a significant improvement under cued-recall versus free-recall conditions. However, healthy preadolescent and teenage examinees show little difference between cued and free recall.

Long-Delay Recall

Long-Delay Free Recall

Following the short-delay cued-recall trial, there is a delay of 20 min for all CVLT measures before administration of long-delay recall trials (delay is 10 min for the Short Form). During the delay, the examinee is typically tested with nonverbal measures so as to not have interference on delayed recall from other verbally mediated tasks. After the delay, the examinee is asked to recall words from List A again (List A only). As with short-delay free recall, this is done without prior warning and without hearing the list again. The long-delay free-recall condition provides an examination of verbal memory over a longer period of time. Unlike for short-delay free recall, there is no interference from a second list of words. As such, there is no retroactive interference and the recall is more of a pure measure of retrieval memory. Scores from long-delay free recall can be compared to other scores in a few ways. First, long-delay free recall of List A could be lower than the total recall of Trial 5 from the learning trials because of a decay of memory over time. In other words, free recall is lower due to the delay of time (i.e., recall could be different when asked to recall 15 or 16 words immediately after hearing than if recalled 20 min later). However, scores could also be lower because of poor encoding or retrieval, poor use of learning strategies, or poor consolidation into long-term memory storage.

Another consideration in the interpretation of long-delay free recall is the difference between the raw score and the percentage of retained information previously recalled in the learning trials. For instance, if Trial 5 was lower than expected for a healthy adult, say seven words, and the same seven words are recalled at the long-delay free-recall trial, the percentage of retention (also called savings) is 100%. This is normal retention, despite the low learning and free-recall scores. However, if the examinee is successful at learning the list with a high learning score (e.g., 15 items) but then recalls only five items on the long-delay free-recall trial, this is a retention of only 33%, which is quite low for a healthy person. As such, it is prudent to examine the level of recall (i.e., the total recall score) as well as the percentage of retention.

As a general rule of thumb, long-delay free recall and long-delay cued recall should be similar to short-delay free recall and short-delay cued recall. That is, if an examinee did poorly on the short-delay free- and cued-recall measures, they would be reasonably expected to do poorly on long delays. However, an examinee may do better on the long-delay free recall than on Trial 5 or the short-delay free-recall trial due to the introduction of semantic prompting during Short-delay cued recall. Long-delay free recall is the first time the examinee is asked to freely recall the list of words following the introduction of semantic cues; therefore, they may now benefit from the semantic categorization of the words.

Clinical Considerations

The clinical interpretation of long-delay free recall is similar to that of the short-delay free recall. Four separate memory profiles can be considered from the explanation of level of recall and percentage of retention.

Profile 1: This profile occurs when the level of recall is high (i.e., good learning and recall) and the percentage of retention is high (i.e., strong savings). This pattern is often observed in healthy children and adults and indicates good learning and memory.

Profile 2: This profile occurs when the level of recall is low (i.e., low learning and low recall) but the percentage of retention is high (i.e., strong savings). This pattern is often observed in psychiatric disorders and among individuals with subcortical processes, such as Huntington's disease or Parkinson's disease, and indicates poor learning but good retention of information learned.

Profile 3: This profile occurs when the level of recall is very low (i.e., impaired learning) and the percentage of retention is also very low (i.e., low savings). This pattern indicates very poor learning; retention may be low simply because of poor learning or because of rapid decay of the little information recalled in learning trials.

Profile 4: This profile occurs when retention is substantially lower than expected based on relatively intact learning as demonstrated by low long-delay free recall and low percentage of retention (i.e., higher learning and lower retention). This can occur in conditions affecting medial temporal functioning, such as Alzheimer's disease, left-temporal epilepsy, Korsakoff's syndrome, or hippocampal sclerosis, and indicates poor learning and retention. This pattern is potentially related to poor encoding or consolidation to long-term memory.

Long-Delay Cued Recall

Immediately following long-delay free recall, the examinee is asked to recall words from List A based on semantic categorization. Long-delay cued recall is interpreted in a similar fashion to short-delay cued recall, allowing you to examine whether cues help an individual recall information. If an examinee did well on long-delay free recall and had previously done well on short-delay cued recall, the long-delay cued recall may not improve recall. However, substantially better delayed recall with cuing implies that more information was encoded than the individual was able to freely recall. Improvement with semantic cueing can be seen among examinees who failed to use semantic clustering or who were more prone to use serial clustering during the learning trials.

Similar to short-delay cued recall, it is important to examine intrusions on long-delay cued recall. As previously mentioned, intrusion errors or confabulatory responses are more likely to occur in certain clinical conditions and the presence of intrusions can help with differential diagnosis. Individuals with Alzheimer's disease, for example, are more likely to display intrusion errors on cued recall.

Yes/No Recognition

Immediately following the long-delay cued-recall trial, the examinee is read a list of words that includes List A, List B, and other words from neither list. This trial determines if the examinee can correctly discriminate items from List A from all other words. Someone new to memory testing may initially think that the Yes/No recognition trial is inconsequential or provides little information about memory. After all, you already have measures of learning and recall. However, if an examinee has poor recall of the words during the long-delay free-recall trial, this could be from either poor encoding during learning or due to poor retrieval, meaning information was encoded but poorly retrieved. Therefore, it is critical to understanding memory that both free recall and recognition memory are assessed for the same information.

There are multiple scores for recognition memory available for the CVLT but we believe it is best to begin with Total Hits, Total False Positives, and Total Recognition Discriminability. Additional recognition scores are discussed in more detail in the following section. On the CVLT-C, Total Hits reflects the number of words from List A that the examinee accurately recognizes (i.e., correctly says yes to a target word). The number of hits is out of 16 for the CVLT-II and CVLT3 standard and alternate forms; out of 9 for brief/short forms; and out of 15 for CVLT-C. Next, Total False Positives reflects the number of items the examinee said "yes" to that were, in fact, not on List A. By examining Hits versus False Positives, you can determine if the examinee accurately encoded the list of words, even if they struggled to freely recall the words on their own. For instance, if an examinee appeared to acquire an average number of words across the learning trials but then recalled only a fraction of those words during delayed recall, this could be due to an initial inability to integrate words into long-term memory (poor encoding). Conversely, it is possible that encoding was actually very strong but he or she could not successfully pull the word list from memory (poor retrieval). However, if the examinee is then given the Yes/No recognition trial and accurately recognizes most or all of the words, this suggests that encoding, in fact, took place, and the examinee simply needed a cue to prompt recall. In addition, even with a high number of hits, the recognition trial can reveal memory deficits if there are also a high number of false positives. If the examinee correctly says "yes" to the words from List A but also says "yes" to words not from List A, cues did not elicit more accurate information and recognition memory would be considered poor. This is why it is helpful to examine the Total Recognition Discriminability, which compares Hits versus False Positives, and examines whether the examinee could distinguish between target and nontarget words from List A. In fact, Total Recognition Discriminability is the best overall measure of recognition because it takes both hits and false positives into account.

A lower score on the Total Recognition Discriminability Index occurs in three possible scenarios. First, a high hit rate in combination with a high false-positive rate suggests poor discriminability. In this situation, the examinee cannot distinguish targets from non-targets. This often occurs in the face of poor encoding and storage and often involves concurrent intrusions and confabulation. Second, an examinee may have a low number of hits and few false positives, often saying "no" to most items on the Yes/No recognition trial. Again, there is poor discriminability between targets and nontargets. Third, it is possible that the examinee may miss targets and endorse nontargets (low hits and high false positives). These latter two patterns are often seen with poor effort, difficulties maintaining set, cases of severe mental illness with apathy, or in cases of poor memory without confabulation.

The principles behind the Total Recognition Discriminability Index are related to the Total Response Bias score, which provides an assessment of the tendency to endorse a specific response on the Yes/No recognition trial (i.e., saying "yes" on more or all items or saying "no" on most or all items). The CVLT manuals refer to this tendency as either a "no" response bias or a "yes" response bias, but it is also sometimes referred to as a negative or positive response bias. In the interpretive report, the directionality of the raw score informs the direction of bias. Specifically, if the raw score is positive, this indicates a "no" response bias direction. If the raw score is negative, this is a "yes" response bias direction.

Consider the following example of recognition discrimination and response bias. An examinee obtains 14 hits from the possible 16 words, which is an average performance. However, she obtains a high number of false positives, producing a standardized score two standard deviations below the mean. The discriminability score, in this case, was one standard deviation below the mean (low average range), suggesting mild difficulty with distinguishing List A words from other nontarget words. The response bias score indicated a strong tendency to say "yes" for words, regardless of which list they came from.

There are additional possible scores you may consider in the Yes/No Recognition section of the score report. These additional scores are based on the characteristics of the nontargets on the Yes/No Recognition trial. In addition to the target words from List A, all the words from List B are included, as well as words from neither list, some of which are semantically related to the lists and some of which are novel words that are not semantically related. Scores that provide detail on the types of foils the examinee selected include:

1. Source recognition discriminability: This score provides a measure of the examinee's ability to distinguish List A words from List B words. Deficits are typically related to poor source memory. In this situation you may also need to determine if the examinee

fully understands the task. You can repeat the instructions, stressing *the list I read to you 5 times* or you can ask the examinee after completing the trial to indicate what they were saying yes to during the task.

2. Semantic recognition discriminability: This is a measure of the examinee's ability to distinguish List A words from words that are semantically related. A poor score here is often correlated to semantic or categorical intrusions on recall trials.
3. Novel recognition discriminability: This is a measure of the examinee's ability to distinguish the 16 target words from List A from novel, nonsemantically related words. This score is often reduced for those with severe memory deficits and low scores on this scale often predict low scores on all other discriminability measures.

The raw score for the discriminability scores noted previously is listed as a d' score (d prime). This raw score calculation is sometimes confusing to both novice and seasoned clinicians. It reflects the standard *z*-score difference between signal to noise (discriminability), where signal refers to hits and noise refers to false positives. For instance, if the examinee's total hits score was 1 standard deviation above the mean ($z = +1.0$) and their false positives score was 1 standard deviation below the mean ($z = -1.0$), these scores would be two standard deviations apart with better performance for hits than false positives. Here, d′ would be 2.0 (mean score difference in *z*-scores between signal and noise). Conversely, a d′ score could be a negative value if the hits standard score was low (−1.0) and the false-positives score was high (+1.0). In this case, d′ would be −2.0.

To this point, we have elaborated on interpretation of primary aspects of the CVLT in order to get a general sense of learning and memory. Depending on the case, you may want to examine finer details of test performance. This is not always necessary. For instance, if your examinee demonstrates strong learning, retention, and recall, and if cognitive abilities are assessed to be within expectation in other areas, there may be little need to explore memory in any additional detail. However, in the presence of diminished performance on the CVLT, it is prudent to ask why performance was reduced. One important advantage ofthe CVLT over other memory tests is that it allows for examining learning characteristics that can assist with differential diagnosis. In the next section, we provide you the tools you need to interpret scores that go beyond the basic aspects of general learning and memory.

LEARNING CHARACTERISTICS

The CVLT provides several scores and analyses that break down the examinee's learning characteristics. These include semantic clustering, serial clustering, subjective clustering (CVLT-II), recency and primacy effects, learning slope, and recall consistency. This section describes each of these scores in detail.

Clustering

Semantic Clustering

During the administration of the CVLT, the examinee may or may not use different learning strategies to acquire more words across trials. Studies demonstrate that immediate memory and learning can be improved by the use of strategies or mnemonic devices (more on this in Chapter 6). As noted in earlier chapters, the word list for each version of the CVLT contains latent semantic groupings (e.g., modes of transportation, articles of clothing). A semantic clustering score is calculated to determine if the examinee recognizes the semantic groupings and uses the groupings to recall items from the list. Remembering three or four categories is less demanding than freely recalling unrelated items; a semantic group provides an "anchor" for the examinee to recall words. Semantic clustering is assumed to occur when the examinee provides consecutively recalled items from a semantic group (i.e., recalling animal words together). During administration, the CVLT word lists are presented in such a way that each item is never followed by an item from the same semantic group. Thus, semantic clustering represents an intentional organization of the word list when recalled.

Serial Clustering

Serial clustering refers to the tendency to recall the word list items in the same order in which they were presented. A serial clustering score is derived across all learning trials. Whereas semantic clustering suggests more engagement and strategic planning, serial clustering is generally associated with a more dysexecutive learning style. Semantic organization can aid in recall whereas serial clustering may be more effortful, thus exhausting effort in learning. This is analogous to chunking in a digit span task. For example, it is much easier to recall 579-823-214 than it is to recall 5-7-9-8-2-3-2-1-4.

Scores for serial clustering are provided as raw scores and standardized scores. There are two different scores for serial clustering, a forward score and a bidirectional score. The Serial Clustering Forward scores represents the examinee's recall of the word list in the same order it was given. However, the CVLT also provides a bidirectional score based on the observation that some examinees will initially provide words from the recency (end of list) section in reverse order and then the primacy (beginning of list) in the forward order. The Serial Clustering Bidirectional score provides an assessment of this possible behavior.

Clinical Considerations of Semantic Versus Serial Clustering

Semantic clustering scores can be dependent on several factors. In general, the use of semantic clustering aids learning and subsequent delayed recall. Lower semantic clustering scores are predictive of worse overall CVLT performance and higher semantic clustering is correlated with higher executive functioning. Those who utilize serial clustering, however, tend to be more stimulus bound and reduced executive functioning is associated with increased use of serial clustering. Clinically, those with executive deficits or difficulties in planning and organizing (e.g., frontal-subcortical conditions, such as Parkinson's or Huntington's disease) may use serial clustering more often than semantic clustering. Several lines of research also demonstrate that women are more likely to use semantic clustering while men are more likely to use serial clustering (Fiszdon, Silverstein, Buchwald, Hull, & Smith, 2003; Lundervold, Wollschläger, & Wehling, 2014; Ragland, Coleman, Gur, Glahn, & Gur, 2000; Sunderaraman, Blumen, DeMatteo, Apa, & Cosentino, 2013).

Similarly, studies of the CVLT-C standardization sample demonstrate that girls are more likely to use semantic clustering than boys (Kramer et al., 1997). Independent of sex, older adults are less likely to demonstrate semantic clustering on the CVLT-II and CVLT3. There is also a clear developmental curve in the use of semantic clustering. Semantic clustering begins to emerge around ages 9–12 and teens use semantic strategies more than 9–12 year-olds and 9–12 year-olds use more semantic strategies than 5–8 year-olds (Kramer et al., 1997).

It is generally assumed that semantic clustering is a higher level skill than serial clustering. As noted, low semantic clustering is correlated with poorer performance on other aspects of the CVLT. Conversely, people with excellent memory may, in fact, have perfect serial recall or may attempt to remember the entire list in serial order to challenge themselves. One of the authors (TJF) tested a particularly gifted individual, an 18-year-old woman, who used the method of loci to learn the CVLT-II words. This method is a common mnemonic device involving spatial visualization. She obtained 16/16 across trials 2–5 and had perfect delayed recall. During a feedback session weeks later, she demonstrated perfect recall of all 16 words and shared that she used this strategy. Certainly, in this case, or similar cases, neither a low semantic clustering score nor a very high serial clustering score is interpreted as problematic.

CAUTION 4.4

Although low semantic clustering is typically indicative of lower executive functioning ability and poor recall, an idiosyncratic approach to encoding and recalling words may also result in low semantic clustering with high memory ability.

Subjective Clustering

There are times when an examinee fails to demonstrate either semantic or serial clustering but employs some type of idiosyncratic learning strategy. The CVLT-II provides a score for subjective clustering across Trials 2–5. Subjective clustering occurs when serial and semantic clustering scores are low but the examinee uses his or her own learning style consistently. Examinees may, for example, pair words together that begin with the same sound or letter (e.g., cow, cabbage, cabinet) or form unique associations or visualizations between words (e.g., visualizing a cow eating lettuce). The CVLT-II manual provides the example of "squirrel, spinach, cow, cabbage," suggesting that each animal could eat the related vegetable exhibiting a phonemic clustering in which words beginning with the same letter are clustered. The subjective clustering score is derived in a similar fashion to the other clustering scores (see Chapter 3). The raw score ranges from −1.88 to 13.13, with higher scores suggesting subjective clustering across trials. High subjective clustering occurs with both high and low total learning scores on Trials 1–5. However, when Trials 1–5 Total Correct score is high, the examinee may have used an effective, idiosyncratic learning style.

Learning Slope

The CVLT-II and CVLT3 provide standardized scores for each learning trial. This allows you to examine recall across learning trials. Although the CVLT-C provides a Trial 1 score, a Trial 5 score, and a total learning score for Trials 1–5, it does not provide standardized individual trial scores for Trials 2–4 (you may still examine performance across learning trials by looking at the raw scores on all learning trials). Fortunately, all CVLT tests include a measure that quantifies an examinee's learning slope. As noted, the learning slope is a measure of the average number of new words gained on recall across subsequent learning trials and reflects the rate of learning. For the CVLT-C, a learning slope of 2 suggests that the child gained an average of 2 additional words on each repeated trial. For example, if Trial 1 was 5 and the learning slope was 2, we would expect that the child would recall 2 additional words on each subsequent learning trial for a total recall of 14 words by Trial 5.

On CVLT-II and CVLT3, a learning slope metric is provided for Trials 1–5 and Trials 2–5, which allows for examination of a change in learning from different points of the test (i.e., Trial 2–5 learning slope removes the first trial, reducing the impact of attention and working memory on slope). One drawback from the learning slope metric on the CVLT-C is that it does not identify the recall across each learning trial like the CVLT-II and CVLT3. The digital scoring program for CVLT-C provides a raw score for Trials 1–5, along with the percentage correct out of 15 words, but there is not a standardized score associated with trials 2–4.

Rapid Reference 4.3

Clinical Considerations in Learning Slope

- The large number of words on the first trial may be anxiety provoking to certain patient groups because the length of the word list is unknown. An increase in anxiety could interfere with performance. On subsequent trials, performance may improve after learning the list is finite and the learning slope metric could provide insight into their learning pattern.
- Individuals with frontal lobe damage may exhibit difficulties with executive functioning that result in a pattern of testing characterized by normal learning in early trials but a quick plateau in learning on trials 3–5. For example, raw scores across Trials 1–5 of 6, 8, 9, 9, and 10.
- Individuals with encoding deficits may never be able to acquire more information than their working memory capacity. These individuals often display a flat learning slope (see the discussion of Alzheimer's disease in Chapter 6).
- Some individuals with retrieval deficits may display poor acquisition across all learning trials as reflected in low learning trial standard scores, and yet they may exhibit a normal learning slope. This is demonstrated by low scores on early trials but a normal rate of learning (see the discussion of Parkinson's disease in Chapter 6). For example, raw scores across Trials 1–5 of 4, 5, 6, 7, and 8.

Recall Order Effects

Primacy and Recency Recall Scores

Individuals tend to recall items from the beginning and end of a list more easily than items from the middle. This well-known phenomenon is referred to as the serial position effect. The serial position effect can be visualized as a U-shaped serial position curve. The theory of this phenomenon holds that two separate memory systems are used to recall items from the list, long-term memory (after the information is successfully encoded) and short-term memory. As the examinee hears the words over multiple trials in the same order, he or she will have more time to rehearse and encode items from the beginning of the list. However, the list is too long for most individuals to encode the entire list using just rehearsal. As such, items in the middle tend to drop out; however, items at the end of the list are more easily recalled as they were most recently heard and remain in working memory. That is, items recalled from the beginning of the list are more likely encoded into long-term memory, items at the end of the list benefit from the capacity of working memory, but those items in the middle exceed the maximum encoding to long-term memory capacity and are too far from the end of the list to benefit from the capacity of working memory.

These basic observations of human memory processing are examined in the CVLT with Primacy, Middle, and Recency Recall Scores. Specifically, the CVLT allows for examination of recall from different sections of the original list—the beginning, middle, and end. The order in which examinees recall words from the original list can provide important clinical information about learning and memory based on learning theory. Primacy effects occur when an individual recalls more words from the beginning of the list. Recency effects occur when an individual recalls words from the end of the list more readily. When an individual recalls more words from the beginning of the list, he or she is exhibiting a strong primacy effect. Conversely, if more words are recalled from the end of the list, the individual is exhibiting strong recency effects. There are meaningful differences in the clinical interpretation of these different learning styles.

The CVLT measures an individual's ability to successfully encode verbal information over multiple trials. Based on learning theory, those with stronger learning and memory abilities will display primacy effects and will even recall several words from the middle over subsequent trials. Stronger scores for primacy and middle items are correlated to better overall learning and recall of the CVLT. Note that younger children are less likely to recall words from the middle of the list compared to their preadolescent and teenage counterparts.

Upon hearing 9, 15, or 16 items from the word list, individuals with poor memory may rely on passive working memory to quickly repeat words from the end of the list. The rapid use of short-term memory does not require the individual to encode information into long-term memory. In fact, low recall of items from the beginning of the list may suggest poor encoding. Recency effects may be more noticeable in individuals with rapid forgetting or difficulty integrating items from the beginning of the list into long-term memory. For example, individuals with Alzheimer's disease are prone to stronger recency effects and weaker primacy effects because of difficulty encoding items at the beginning of

CAUTION 4.5

A low primacy effect score does not indicate whether poor recall was from reduced encoding or retrieval. Poor recall may be due to a deficit in encoding or retrieval. For example, individuals with subcortical dementias (e.g., Parkinson's disease dementia or Huntington's disease) may display poor primacy effects and poor recall but may still have normal recognition memory, suggesting that the memory difficulties are related to reduced retrieval and not storage.

the list. CVLT-C normative data indicate that younger children are more likely to exhibit recency effects compared to preadolescents and teenagers who are more likely to exhibit primacy effects.

Recall Consistency

CVLT provides a Recall Consistency score, the percentage of target words recalled once on a trial that are then subsequently recalled on the next trial. The recall consistency score provides insight into whether the examinee is using the same strategy across trials. Low recall consistency may simply reflect limited learning capacity; individuals with poor learning may abandon one strategy for another or not utilize an effective strategy. For example, an individual may focus on later items on the first few trials and then shift focus to earlier items in an effort to obtain more items from the beginning of the list on later trials. Similar to other scores, recall consistency scores exhibit a developmental progression. That is, teenagers are more likely to be consistent in their recall compared to preadolescents and preadolescents are more consistent than younger children. Individuals with poorer executive functioning, such as those with frontal lobe lesions, may respond to each trial as if it is the first time that they have heard the word list and use a different strategy each time. This approach will result in a low Recall Consistency score across trials. Inconsistent recall is often observed in those with attentional deficits, such as those with moderate to severe ADHD.

Rapid Reference 4.4

Relevant Definitions

- Semantic Clustering: Recalling words together that are categorically related (i.e., animals or vegetables grouped together).
- Serial Clustering: Recalling the words in the same serial order in which they were presented.
- Primacy: The tendency to recall words from the beginning of the list.
- Recency: The tendency to recall words from the end of the list.
- Middle: The recall of the middle words.
- Learning Slope: The average number of new words gained on recall across learning trials. This is thought to reflect the rate of learning.
- Recall Consistency: The percentage of target words that are recalled once on each trial that are then subsequently recalled again on the next trial.

Trials 2–5 Total Correct

An incremental improvement across trials or a positive learning curve is expected in healthy individuals when they are given additional opportunities to learn a string of information. The examinee is no longer relying solely on working memory; rather, they are using working memory but also retrieving words from long-term storage in order to recall more words across trials. The learning curve is central to examining the verbal learning abilities of the examinee and the learning and recall performances measured on Trials 2–5 provide several clinically significant data points. For CVLT-II and CVLT3, standardized scores are provided for each trial, which allows you to examine the presence of learning. Given that a learning curve is expected in healthy individuals (again, with the exception of those who ceiling out early), a drop in standard scores in the third or fourth trial may inform the clinician that the examinee had a brief lapse in attention or motivation.

Rapid Reference 4.5

Learning Slope

The rate of learning is measured by the learning slope score not the individual trial scores, but it is good clinical practice to look at both the individual trials and the learning slope score. Consistency of recall is measured in the recall consistency score. Trials 2–5 learning slope score allows you to look at learning slope without the impact of attention.

RECALL ERRORS

All versions of the CVLT assess errors made during recall. This includes repetitions and intrusions. There are different types of repetitions and intrusions, and a careful examination of these errors can provide valuable clinical information regarding the examinee's memory performance. Note that the CVLT-C uses the term Perseverations; however, CVLT-II and CVLT3 use the term Repetitions.

Repetitions and Perseverations

A repetition is repeating a word already provided *within* any given recall trial. For instance, a child says *bananas* once on a recall trial but then repeats the word again on the same trial. These errors may reflect perseverative tendencies; however, not all repetitions should be thought of as perseverative. Repetitions may also represent difficulties in source memory; the examinee may recall the word but not recall who said it most recently (examinee or examiner). Difficulties with source memory are observed in children with certain developmental conditions, fetal alcohol spectrum disorders, intellectual disability, or in children or adults with frontal lobe pathology. Repetitions may also be related to difficulties in attention and concentration. Lapses in attention during recall will increase the rate of repetitions.

It is important not to consider words said as self-cues as repetitions. Examinees may recite words multiple times as a prompt to elicit further words; however, the examinee is not intending these to be additional responses. If it is unclear whether a repeated word is a self-cue, you can ask the examinee to clarify using the prompts discussed in Chapter 3.

On the CVLT, Total Repetitions are tracked and the interpretive report will provide a raw score and a standardized score. The CVLT C describes these scores as perseverations. The CVLT-C and CVLT-II utilize the *z*-score for the standard score, whereas the CVLT3 uses a scaled score.

Intrusions

An intrusion is a word that is not part of the list the examinee is being asked to recall. Intrusions can reflect different types of memory problems. In general, a high number of intrusions is a sign of significant memory problems and difficulties distinguishing the relevance of word responses. Those with Alzheimer's disease and Korsakoff syndrome are particularly vulnerable to higher intrusion rates. Individuals with Down syndrome are also more likely to exhibit high intrusion rates. A close examination of intrusions may provide insight into the examinee's memory abilities. It is best to start investigating intrusions with the Total Intrusions score before examining subtypes of intrusions. This score includes all intrusions, regardless of type, given by the examinee on all recall trials. If this number is very low, then all other intrusion scores will also be low. If this number is high, then a more detailed examination of intrusions will serve to elucidate the types of errors made by the examinee. One caveat to interpreting intrusions: if the words are phonetically similar to target words it may suggest hearing difficulties. The CVLT interpretive report provides a raw score and standard score for all intrusion types.

After examining total intrusions, you should examine where the intrusions occurred. The CVLT provides a differentiation of total intrusions for immediate recall (Trials 1–5), delayed recall (free recall and cued recall), total free recall (immediate and delayed free recall), and total cued-recall trials. In this way, you can see where intrusions occurred. For instance, a 65-year-old male obtained a Total Intrusion raw score of 6 on the CVLT-II. However, all of the intrusions occurred on the cued-recall trials, suggesting the category prompts may have resulted in confabulatory responses.

Rapid Reference 4.6

Intrusion Types

The exact type of intrusion can be helpful to note.

1. Synonym/subordinate intrusions: an intrusion that is closely related to one of the words from the list. For example, instead of "bookcase," the examinee provides "book-shelf." A subordinate intrusion error describes additional exemplars of a target word (e.g., rather than onion, the examinee provides yellow onion, green onion, or red onion).

Synonym and subordinate intrusions are considered to be relatively minor compared to other intrusion types and typically reflect difficulties in attention.

2. Across-List intrusions: intrusions that are the recall of a List A word during List B recall or a List B word during List A recall. These types of intrusions are considered more problematic than the synonym/subordinate errors and reflect deficits in source memory. These errors also suggest proactive and retroactive interference, which were discussed previously.
3. Categorical Intrusions are incorrect responses that are semantically related to the target lists and reflect semantic errors, such as recalling furniture or fruits that were not on List A. These semantic-type errors may be related to confabulatory responses, and higher rates of categorical intrusions are negatively correlated with Yes/No recognition hits.
4. Noncategory Intrusions, or novel words not associated with either list, reflect a more serious memory problem. High rates of noncategory intrusions are associated with more pronounced memory deficits, as well as possible deficits in other cognitive domains, such as complex attention or language processing.

DON'T FORGET 4.4

For the primary learning and recall trials, a higher *z*-score indicates better performance. However, on the CVLT-C and CVLT-II, for the recency-recall index and the error scores, higher *z*-scores suggest worse performance.

The CVLT provides several comparisons of intrusions across different trials. These comparisons are called recall discriminability scores and provide further analysis of how the examinee performed across the test. For example, a higher rate of intrusions on the five learning trials relative to the delayed recall trials suggests that the examinee may have trouble with inhibiting verbal responses due to the recency of hearing the words read by the examiner. However, those with stronger attention skills but poor recall may be able to initially inhibit intrusions on learning trials, but then exhibit intrusions during delayed recall. The recall discriminability scores compare the following trials:

1. Total-Recall Discriminability: All trials of List A versus total intrusions
2. Immediate-Recall Discriminability: Trials 1–5 of List A versus intrusions from List A
3. Delayed-Recall Discriminability: List A total versus Delayed-Recall Intrusions
4. Free-Recall Discriminability: List A total versus immediate- and delayed-recall trials
5. Cued-Recall Discriminability: List A total versus intrusions from the cued-recall trials

PERFORMANCE VALIDITY (CVLT-II AND CVLT3)

As with all psychological and cognitive test instruments, interpretability is dependent on the validity of the data. There are many reasons a test protocol could be rendered invalid. Some reasons may be related to examiner errors, such as a mistake on test administration. Validity may also be reduced due to factors related to the examinee. We caution, however, that reduced performance validity markers on the CVLT should not be viewed as diagnostic of malingering or suboptimal effort. Although malingering may certainly play a role for some examinees, other factors could also interfere with performance, such as severe pain or illness, delirium, active psychosis, active substance use, or medication effects. Of course, in best clinical practice, you would screen for such factors before determining if the examinee is even amenable to testing.

After the Yes/No Recognition trial, there is a built in delay before the Forced-Choice Recognition Trial, which is listed as an optional trial. Here, each of the original List A items is presented with another paired word the examinee has not yet been exposed to, and the examinee is asked to choose which of the two words was from the first list. The non-target words are thought of as being in stark contrast to the original words. As such, even if the examinee did not do well on recall measures, the target words should stand apart and be easily recognized. The forced-choice recognition trial provides insight into the validity of the CVLT because most individuals perform well on the task. In fact, over 94% of the CVLT-II normative sample obtained a perfect score. On CVLT3, the mean score for all age bands was 15.9 (SD = 0.4). As such, scores below a perfect 16/16 raise concern of reduced validity. Like most performance validity tests that have a dichotomous structure, an examinee should obtain about 50% correct if they were to just guess at random. Therefore, scores at or below chance-level responding are suspect for a disingenuous presentation and possible feigned impairment. Conversely, although missing one or two items may not be clinically meaningful, it is more common in those with an apathetic presentation or in an amnestic individual. Forced-Choice Correct Hits is the total number of correctly identified target words. The interpretive report then provides the percentage of the normative sample that had the same score and the cumulative percentage of the normative sample that scored better. In the example of a perfect 16/16 (100%), 94.5% of the CVLT-II sample had the same score and 0% had higher (cannot have a score higher than 16). Similarly, 91.4% of the CVLT3 sample had a perfect score.

In addition to the Forced-Choice Recognition trial, the CVLT-II and CVLT3 also provide a critical item analysis, which can further elucidate reduced effort.

1. The first critical item assesses how many items were recalled at least once on a recall trial, but were then subsequently missed on the Forced-Choice Recognition trial. This analysis makes a few assumptions about recall and recognition. Why, for example, would a person recall an item but then fail to recognize it later when recall is typically more challenging then recognition? Second, should an examinee be expected to recognize an item if they never seemed to recall it on previous trials? The CVLT provides a raw number of such occurrences and a percentage of how many people from the normative sample had similar scores.
2. Similar to the comparison of recall versus Forced-Choice Recognition, the second critical item analysis provides a comparison of how many items were recognized on the Yes/No Recognition Trial that were subsequently missed on Forced Choice. Again, this assumes that it would be unusual to correctly identify an item on Yes/No and then miss the same item later on an ostensibly easier trial. Again, the output reflects a raw number of such occurrences and a percentage of how many people from the normative sample had similar scores.

In practice, it is prudent and helpful to consider the Forced-Choice Recognition scores as well as the Critical Items analysis when assessing performance validity. The CVLT-II and CVLT3 do not provide definitive cut scores for performance validity and some degree of clinical judgment is typically required. We recommend careful consideration of additional cognitive measures, clinical history, and current symptomatology before making statements about effort.

It is our hope that with careful practice and utilization of this text, as well as the original manuals, you will increase your interpretive skills for the CVLT. In later chapters, we provide a discussion of specific conditions and diseases and how individuals with such conditions typically perform on the CVLT.

TEST YOURSELF

1. **Which of the following factors should always be considered in assessing the validity of the CVLT test results?**
   (a) Expressive/receptive language
   (b) English language proficiency
   (c) Mental status
   (d) Hearing function
   (e) All of the above
2. **When considering demographic factors, age, education, and sex appear more influential to CVLT test performance than race or ethnicity.**
   True
   False
3. **For a z-score of 1.5, find the equivalent score below.**
   (a) *T* of 65
   (b) *T* of 60
   (c) Standard score of 130
   (d) Scaled score of 13
4. **Which of the following represents proactive interference on the CVLT?**
   (a) The supraspan nature of the word list makes it difficult to retain more items than working memory will allow.
   (b) Items learned on List A interfere with the examinee's ability to retain words from List B.
   (c) List B learning interferes with recall on the short-delay recall trial.
   (d) The examinee displays poor savings as reflected in a low percentage of items recalled at the long-delay free-recall trial.
5. **What type of testing patterns would be expected for individuals with a subcortical/dysexecutive pattern on the CVLT (e.g., Parkinson's disease)?**
   (a) Diminished acquisition, with low recall, but clear improvement on cueing and recognition formats.

(b) A flat learning curve, with impaired recall and impaired recognition.
(c) High levels of learning and high levels of recall but reduced recognition due to impaired attention.
(d) A significant amount of confabulation on cued-recall trials.

6. What might it imply if an examinee is able to recall more items after cueing than he or she could on free recall?

(a) The examinee is amnestic.
(b) The examinee is displaying confabulation that interferes with recall.
(c) The examinee has deficits in retrieval but has adequate encoding.
(d) It does not imply anything until you verify the problem with Yes/No recognition.

7. What is learned from the Total Recognition Discriminability score?

(a) The score provides the probability that the examinee was putting forth poor effort on the test.
(b) The score provides an analysis of how often the examinee recalled semantically related words.
(c) The score provides a standardized score of how many Hits the examinee had relative to the standardization sample.
(d) The score compares Hits versus False Positives to determine if the examinee could distinguish targets from nontargets.

8. Total Response Bias provides the examiner with what type of information?

(a) Any trends in Yes/No responding, such as favoring "yes" more than would be expected (i.e., positive response bias).
(b) The score provides the probability that the examinee was putting forth poor effort on the test.
(c) The score provides a standardized score of how many Hits the examinee had relative to the standardization sample.
(d) There is a significant amounts of confabulation on cued-recall trials.

9. An above-average score on semantic clustering implies what about the examinee's performance?

(a) They were more likely to recall words in the same order in which the examiner read them.
(b) They were more likely to recall words from the end of the list.
(c) They were more likely to recall words based on latent semantic categories.
(d) They were more likely to recall words from the beginning of the list.

10. Men are more likely to use semantic clustering than women.

True
False

11. Older children are more likely to use semantic clustering than younger children.

True
False

12. How is the serial position effect measured in the CVLT?

(a) Learning slope scores.

(b) Total learning score.

(c) Recency and primacy effects.

(d) Response bias scores.

13. ______ is to short-term storage as ______ is to long-term storage.

14. Which patient group is more like to display intrusion errors?

(a) Huntington's disease.

(b) Alzheimer's disease.

(c) ADHD.

(d) Stroke patients.

15. Forced-Choice Recognition is a measure of what?

(a) Delayed recall.

(b) Learning consistency.

(c) The number of items recalled at least once that were then missed on Yes/No recognition.

(d) A measure of performance validity.

Answers: 1. e, 2. True, 3. a, 4. b, 5. a. 6. c, 7. d, 8. a, 9. c, 10. False, 11. True, 12. c, 13. Recency, Primacy, 14. b, 15. d

Five

STRENGTHS AND WEAKNESSES OF CVLT

The California Verbal Learning Test (CVLT) offers a comprehensive evaluation of verbal learning and memory. It has been widely researched and used extensively with clinical populations across the lifespan. Moreover, it is a frequently used tool to assess change in memory functioning over time. Despite the widespread acceptance and use of the instrument, there are limitations of its use that you should consider when administering the CVLT. This chapter discusses the strengths and weaknesses of the CVLT overall and within each of the three editions.

CVLT STRENGTHS AND WEAKNESSES

The CVLT provides an extensive evaluation of verbal learning and memory within a relatively short memory measure. It is deeply rooted in the process approach theory of assessment and provides detailed information on the learning strategies and styles of examinees and covers nearly the entire lifespan. Normative data are provided on many unique aspects of memory that originated with the CVLT, many of which have been incorporated into other memory measures. The ability to continually break down performance into various subprocesses provides a unique insight into an individual's memory deficits and treatment options.

Each edition of CVLT exhibits good psychometric properties on the primary variables. Reliability is high for the primary scores and the validity is established both within the initial validity studies reported in the manual and in research utilizing the CVLT in numerous populations, ages, and diagnoses. There are over 5,000 studies that have utilized a version of the CVLT in relation to diagnostic accuracy, treatment efficacy, progress monitoring, and memory research. It has been used in studies on various disorders including Down syndrome, nonverbal learning disorders, multiple sclerosis, Parkinson's disease, Alzheimer's dementia, depression, and anxiety. See Chapter 6 for an overview of the literature on the clinical utility of the CVLT. This deep research library, collected in various clinical populations, allows you to find relevant literature to help understand and interpret an individual's performance on the CVLT when they are part of one of the researched clinical populations. Further, the research supports the use of the primary scores and many of the secondary process scores; some secondary scores have mixed support or no research support and need further investigation.

Some of the strengths of the CVLT relate to its weaknesses. The comprehensiveness of the evaluation produces a large number of scores that can be overwhelming to score and interpret, particularly to a new user. While this manual describes an approach to interpretation, the sheer number of scores that need to be calculated, integrated, and interpreted is daunting. Scoring can take a long period of time and is prone to error due to the complexity and number of calculations. Computerized scoring aids in this but is not feasible in all clinical settings or for all examiners. In addition, the number of scores can lead to focused use of only the primary scores, which limits the clinical utility and data richness of the CVLT. Alternately, it can also encourage overinterpretation of a single low score. It is important not to overestimate the importance of a single variable within the array of scores provided on CVLT but to view low performance within the context of related scores and the general context of overall cognitive functioning.

The number of possible process scores also makes the CVLT unique. Although many list-learning tests exist, the structure of the CVLT, with embedded semantic categories and an interference list, provides scores related to interference, clustering, and effort that are not available with other similar tests. These additional scores capture data on memory processes but also on other cognitive skills that affect memory, such as attention and executive functioning. However, reliability for many of the process scores is difficult to estimate or is low and there is no research support for the clinical utility of all the variables that can be derived and learning and interpreting all of the variables and how they interrelate takes time and practice.

Rapid Reference 5.1

Strengths and Weaknesses of the CVLT

Strengths	Weaknesses
Extensive evaluation of verbal learning and memory	Only verbal domain assessed
Large, representative normative samples	Overwhelming array of scores
Theoretically based approach	Lengthy to hand calculate all scores
Normative data on multiple measures	Some measures not supported psychometrically
Good psychometric properties on primary measures	Variability in scores across versions
Large research support in clinical populations	

Although CVLT provides many scores, it directly evaluates only verbal learning and memory; this limits diagnostic information to this sensory modality. Modifications that may assist individuals with hearing or language differences are outside of the standardized administration and reduce the applicability of the normative data. Finally, the variability in the scoring across editions makes comparisons across versions difficult. For example, an examiner who assesses a 15-year-old with the CVLT-C and then reassesses him 2 years later with the CVLT3 will be restricted in what comparisons in performance they can directly make across the instruments. Although the CVLT-II and CVLT3 utilize the same word lists, the methods used to derive raw scores differ across the two instruments. This is why it is recommended that the same instrument used in the initial assessment be used for retest purposes as well. Because alternate forms are available for ages 16–90, the same instrument can be used across assessments while minimizing the influence or experience with the previous word lists.

STRENGTHS AND WEAKNESSES OF THE CVLT-C

The CVLT-C is the oldest of the three current editions and does not benefit from the additional research incorporated into the score derivations and structure used in the CVLT-II and CVLT3. It shares the same theoretical base and comprehensive format as the other instruments but utilizes a unique administration with the inclusion of a framework around the recall of the word lists, namely the Monday and Tuesday shopping lists. It utilized a good, representative sample at the time and has good reliability and validity support for the primary scores and some process scores. Like with all three instruments, some of the process scores demonstrate lower reliabilities and should be regarded and interpreted with caution. The CVLT-C has been used extensively in pediatric memory research and has a large research support base.

Another strength of the CVLT-C comes from the fact that the normative data have provided the field of pediatric assessment a basis for understanding how learning, memory, and learning strategies differ as a product of age, maturation, and sex. This developmental data has shaped how the field understands normal and abnormal memory in various pediatric conditions.

The major weakness of the CVLT-C is its age. The sample collected for the CVLT-C was stratified using data collected in 1988. The population of children today is quite different from this stratification and new norms are sorely needed. The content of the word lists likely also needs to be updated as some of the words may have changed in frequency of use from the creation of the lists. The use of the framing around the word lists has also been questioned; it is not clear if the concept of shopping lists is a common experience for children, particularly those in the lower age range of the scale (Ogletree, 1998).

Two editions of the CVLT have been published since the CVLT-C; therefore, the structure and scores have been updated with guidance from reviews and research. However, the CVLT-C has not benefited from these updates. It does not contain an alternate form or a brief form; of course, the standard form is shorter on the CVLT-C so a brief form may not be as clinically useful as it is on the adult forms. In addition, the CVLT-C does not include Forced-Choice Recognition or any other form of performance validity. Lichtenstein, Erdodi, and Linnea (2017) introduced a forced-choice recognition trial that can be added to the CVLT-C administration as a performance validity measure and there is growing support for its use (Lichtenstein, Holcomb, & Erdodi, 2018). Others have also suggested other internal measures to assess performance validity with the CVLT-C (e.g., Baker, Connery, Kirk, & Kirkwood, 2014; Brooks & Ploetz, 2015) but none of these are included within the published manual or software.

Individual trial norms are not available on the CVLT-C and savings scores are based on differences in scaled scores instead of in raw scores. In addition, many of the intrusion and recognition analyses are not provided on the CVLT-C. Also, some of the scores are computed differently than in later editions. Although the software improves the time required to calculate scores, the software is old and incompatible with many current systems. Q-interactive administration provides many of the scores but only a subset of those that can be calculated.

Rapid Reference 5.2

Strengths and Weaknesses of the CVLT-C

Strengths	Weaknesses
Anchors the word lists in shopping paradigm	Shopping paradigm may not be appropriate for all children
Word lists are designed for children	Word lists need updating
Extensive research in pediatric populations	Old normative data based on outdated demographic data
Extensive verbal memory evaluation in youngest ages (not reduced in scope from older ages)	No alternate or short forms
Research based performance validity indicators post publication	Does not match score structure of the adult versions
Digital administration	No measure of performance validity
Inclusion on Q-interactive software allows digital administration	Calculation of some scores is inconsistent with newer approaches
CLVT scores can be substituted for WMS-IV scores	Old scoring software

STRENGTHS AND WEAKNESSES OF THE CVLT-II

The CVLT-II was the first revision of the CVLT for adults and updated the administration and scoring. It dropped the shopping framework around the word lists and modified scoring approaches based on feedback from users and researchers. It added alternate and short forms and measures of performance validity. A large, representative sample was collected for norming and the primary variables have strong psychometric support. The manual provides detail on hand calculating most scores, although the time to hand calculate is still lengthy, and a user-friendly, comprehensive computer-scoring program was provided.

Due to the age of the software, it may not work on newer systems but some scores are available through digital administration on Q-interactive. One unique aspect of the CVLT-II is the ability to substitute CVLT-II scores for the Verbal Paired Associates subtest scores on the Wechsler Memory Scale, Fourth Edition (WMS-IV; Wechsler, 2009). This reduces overall testing time when the CVLT-II and WMS-IV are both given within a comprehensive battery, without reducing the comprehensive assessment of memory.

Since the publication of CVLT-II, thousands of studies have been published that support the psychometric properties of the CVLT-II and the validity of the CVLT-II across multiple clinical groups and populations, including psychiatric, neurological, and memory disorders. Similar to the CVLT-C, the major weakness of the CVLT-II is its age. The sample collected for the CVLT-II was stratified using Census data collected in 1999. The demographics of the population have changed since this stratification. The CVLT3 updated scoring approaches based on research since the publication of the CVLT-II; therefore, scores may not align across versions. Some scores are available only through the scoring software; however, the original software is easy to use and produces all the potential variables but is not compatible with newer computer systems. The primary scores and a few secondary scores can be obtained through the digital administration on Q-interactive.

Rapid Reference 5.3

Strengths and Weaknesses of the CVLT-II

Strengths	**Weaknesses**
Extensive research in adult populations	Old normative data based on outdated demographic data
Well-validated measure of performance validity	Calculation of some scores is inconsistent with newer approaches
Provided alternate and short forms	Old scoring software
Inclusion on Q-interactive software allows digital administration	Low reliability for some secondary scores
Detailed information on how to calculate scores	

STRENGTHS AND WEAKNESSES OF THE CVLT3

The CVLT3 is the newest of the CVLT versions for adults and benefits from the extensive research and customer feedback gathered on the CVLT-II. Because the word lists and administration were kept the same as in the CVLT-II, much of the research support gathered using the CVLT-II can be applied to the CVLT3. An exception to this is the forced-choice recognition task; some words were modified in this trial and, therefore, more research is needed to support its use in multiple populations. The CVLT3 retained alternate and short forms as well. A new, representative sample was collected for norming and the primary variables have strong psychometric support. Although the time to hand calculate is still lengthy, the manual provides detailed information on calculating scores and provides alternate methods for scores previously limited to scoring software. All scores are provided on the Q-global platform and digital administration through Q-interactive also provides all scores. Age-based norms are provided in both digital and hand scoring; education and gender adjustments to these scores are provided through the software.

The sample collected for the CVLT3 was stratified using Census data gathered in 2017. Graves et al. (2019) describes the cohort differences observed across the two standardization samples collected for CVLT-II and CVLT3. The differences highlight the importance of using current population norms. A major weakness of the CVLT3 is the lack of concurrent and clinical validity data with the new norms. Given the scoring changes made, new validity data would have enhanced the direct application of the new normative data.

Rapid Reference 5.4

Strengths and Weaknesses of the CVLT3

Strengths	**Weaknesses**
Minimal content changes from CVLT-II	Some words are commonly misrecalled and were not updated
Inclusion of alternate and brief forms	No new clinical data reported
Current normative sample	Minimal research on new scores in literature
Digital administration	Forced choice has slightly more variability in the norms
Inclusion on Q-interactive software allows digital administration	Scoring software is online only
Detailed information on how to calculate scores	

TEST YOURSELF

1. Which of the following represent weaknesses of the CVLT-C?

(a) The age of the test suggests possible cohort effects.

(b) The CVLT-C scoring program is not compatible with newer systems.

(c) The test does not have a built-in performance validity measure

(d) All of the above

2. A unique feature of the CVLT-II is that it can be used in place of the Verbal Paired Associates subtest of the WMS-IV.

True or False

3. What is one possible problem with using the CVLT-II when the CVLT3 is now available for use?

(a) There are cohort differences across time, meaning the performance of a 25-year-old on the CVLT-II may not be the same as it would be for the CVLT3.

(b) The words are the same across tests, so there is no difference in tests.

(c) You should always use the same version at follow-up as was used at baseline.

(d) Standardized scores are more difficult to interpret on the CVLT-II than the CVLT3.

4. What is the main difference between the CVLT-II and CVLT3?

(a) The tests have slight differences on the Forced-Choice Recognition Trial.

(b) The CVLT3 includes a normative update based on 2017 Census data.

(c) Both a and b are correct.

(d) There are no differences between the tests.

Answers: 1. d, 2. True, 3. a, 4. c

Six

CVLT PERFORMANCE IN CLINICAL POPULATIONS

The previous chapters introduced the various editions of the California Verbal Learning Test (CVLT), providing guidance on administering, scoring, and interpreting the various forms and scores. This chapter goes beyond this information to review how particular clinical populations perform on the CVLT, not through individual case studies, which are provided in Chapter 7, but with reviews of studies gathered in groups of individuals with specific clinical diagnoses. The present chapter provides a general overview of expected clinical group performances as a reference for you in your clinical assessments. Knowing how different populations perform on the CVLT allows you to explore the types of score patterns that might emerge in the populations you are assessing.

Given that thousands of published studies using a version of the CVLT have examined memory abilities in dozens of patient groups, an exhaustive review is not possible here. However, the reviews focus on the most common clinical groups referred for memory evaluation. Because the CVLT3 was only recently published (2017), less literature on it is currently available. However, given that the administration is nearly identical in CVLT-II and CVLT3, you can extend CVLT-II literature findings to similar groups being evaluated with the CVLT3 (i.e., patterns of performance in Alzheimer's disease (AD) are likely the same in CVLT-II and CVLT3), with the exception of the Forced-Choice Recognition trial. Although this chapter focuses on the clinical groups' performance, it is important to review Chapter 4 where details on clinical groups' performance within each CVLT score are also described. In addition to the information presented in this chapter, the test manuals provide extensive information on clinical groups' performance. The information is presented first for clinical group performance on the CVLT-II and CVLT3, followed by information for the CVLT-C.

CVLT-II AND CVLT3 IN CLINICAL POPULATIONS

In the adult population, the most frequent uses of the CVLT are to evaluate individuals with suspected memory difficulties, such as memory decline related to insidious disease processes or memory changes due to injury or insult to the central nervous system (CNS), and psychiatric disorders with known memory impairment. The CVLT is almost always used within a larger battery of tests to derive a diagnosis but is an essential part of the memory evaluation.

Memory Decline

In terms of the use of the CVLT with populations experiencing memory decline, the most common usage is in evaluations for dementia as opposed to age-related memory decline. In each evaluation related to concerns of memory decline, it is important to distinguish performance deficits on the CVLT that may be related to a disorder and memory declines related to normal aging. Declines in memory performance related to aging will generally be accommodated for by the use of age-corrected normative scores; lower raw scores are associated with average scores as age increases. The use of additional demographic adjustments to scores can help identify a decline in more highly educated individuals as well on the CVLT3. In general, though, normative scores in the average range of performance do not indicate the presence of a memory deficit; additional clinical evidence needs to be acquired to support an average performance being a decline from preassessment ability.

Although other causes of decline have been identified, the most commonly investigated are AD, Parkinson's disease (PD), and Huntington's disease (HD); therefore, the research on CVLT performance within each of these populations is presented.

Alzheimer's Disease and Amnestic MCI

AD is the most common cause of dementia, with estimates ranging from 50% to 70% of all cases of dementia being due to this disease (Smith & Bondi, 2013). It is considered a cortical dementia affecting brain regions related to memory. Appropriate treatment requires an accurate diagnosis of individuals with suspected AD and numerous studies have demonstrated that the CVLT provides excellent diagnostic sensitivity and specificity for AD. In Chapter 7, a case example is provided of the use of CVLT-II in the clinical assessment of an individual with probable AD. A second case study is available in the CVLT-II manual. Both of these cases illustrate the utility of the CVLT in the assessment of memory and the differential diagnosis of individuals with suspected memory change associated with AD.

Amnestic mild cognitive impairment (aMCI) is a known precursor and risk factor for developing dementia of the Alzheimer's type; individuals with aMCI are more likely to convert to AD than those with other forms of MCI (Smith & Bondi, 2013). Given the similar characteristics and disease progression in aMCI and AD, the following sections outline performance on the CVLT among both individuals with AD and those with aMCI, first covering learning characteristics, followed by recall and recognition abilities.

Learning characteristics Performance patterns and strategies on the initial learning trials provide valuable clinical information about which regions of the brain may be functioning abnormally. This, in turn, can help you form clinical hypotheses about what might be causing any observed impairments. AD is characterized by pathological changes to the medial temporal lobe and hippocampal structure. These regions of the brain are important for long-term memory storage of episodic information. Therefore, examining how individuals acquire information across learning trials can help differentiate normal cognitive functioning from declines due to aMCI and AD.

In studies comparing learning of individuals with either aMCI or AD to healthy controls, individuals with aMCI or AD recalled half the number of words across learning trials as healthy controls (Pike, Rowe, Moss, & Savage, 2008). Individuals with aMCI or AD often display poor learning slope scores, demonstrating a relatively flat learning curve in comparison to healthy older adults. In addition, they display a tendency to recall words from the recency portion of the list, suggesting they echo what was heard most recently because of failure to adequately encode information from the primacy section of the list.

An examination of the strategies used to encode information is also helpful in differentiating aMCI and AD. Semantic clustering, which involves grouping the words in semantic categories to facilitate recall (e.g., recalling *furniture* items together), may be a key indicator of aMCI or AD on CVLT. Individuals with AD are much less likely to use semantic clustering, so much so that scores on semantic clustering differentiated individuals with AD from healthy controls (Delis et al., 2010). It appears that deficits in semantic language functioning are a hallmark characteristic of AD.

Amnestic MCI is often thought of as being a prodromal phase of AD. That is, individuals with aMCI are more likely to progress to AD than other individuals with nonamnestic MCI (Smith & Bondi, 2013). Semantic clustering abilities also differentiate individuals across the continuum of healthy aging to probable AD. McLaughlin et al. (2014) demonstrated that those with a nonamnestic MCI used semantic clustering more frequently across subsequent trials. That is, although individuals with nonamnestic MCI may not have used semantic clustering in early trials, they were more likely to adopt semantic clustering with each subsequent trial. However, those with aMCI and individuals with AD failed to show any change in semantic clustering across trials. Both the aMCI and AD groups demonstrated significantly lower semantic clustering relative to healthy controls but there were no differences between the aMCI and AD groups. This suggests the failure to learn the use of grouping strategies across trials in the aMCI and AD groups. An evaluation of semantic clustering abilities in individuals with MCI may help differentiate subtypes of MCI and suggest who is more likely to develop AD longitudinally.

Taken together, clinical research literature demonstrates that aMCI and AD patient groups often display diminished learning, a flat learning curve, low use of effective learning strategies, and recency effects relative to healthy groups.

Recall abilities Given the pathology observed in the medial temporal lobe of individuals with AD, it is expected that these patient populations will struggle with delayed recall. Multiple studies have identified deficits in both long-delay free and cued recall in aMCI compared to controls (Hutchens et al., 2012; Lee et al., 2016). Given the expected decline in recall, retention is also expected to be low. Healthy controls demonstrate an average savings of approximately 70% whereas individuals with aMCI display a savings of approximately 50% and individuals with AD display a savings of approximately 5% (Pike et al., 2008). These findings reflect a rapid forgetting of the word list because information is not encoded. In simple terms, the information has nowhere to go for storage and is therefore not retained, recalled, or recognized to the same level as it is in healthy groups.

Recognition memory is an important part of a dementia evaluation, particularly when you are trying to distinguish AD from other forms of dementia. Because of deficits in medial temporal lobe functioning, individuals with AD show deficits in encoding that result in difficulties with recognition memory on the CVLT. Pike et al. (2008) found that healthy controls show 93% accuracy, those with aMCI show 67% accuracy, and individuals with AD show 63% accuracy on Yes/No recognition. Amnestic MCI and AD groups were indistinguishable from each other on all primary recognition scores, including recognition hits, false positives, and response bias.

The CVLT is particularly useful in differential diagnosis and determining which individuals are at risk of additional cognitive decline longitudinally. Multiple studies have demonstrated that learning and recall aspects of the CVLT-II help distinguish healthy individuals from individuals with MCI (Bilgel et al., 2014; Parikh et al., 2014; Silva et al., 2012). Rabin et al. (2009) used logistic regression to demonstrate that performance on CVLT-II Total Learning successfully differentiated individuals with MCI from healthy controls, with a sensitivity of 90% and a specificity of 84%. Rabin and colleagues followed up with participants approximately 3 years later and found that MCI patients with lower baseline scores on CVLT-II were more likely to convert to AD, with Long-Delay Free Recall being the best predictor of who would develop AD. Pozueta et al. (2011) also used a 2-year longitudinal design to examine whether performance on the CVLT predicted which patients with MCI converted to AD. The sample included 115 older adults, 50 of whom converted to AD across the study time frame. Analysis of CVLT performance demonstrated that lower abilities at baseline, particularly on short and long-delay recall trials, were predictive of which individuals would develop AD with an accuracy of approximately 94%.

In summary, the CVLT is a useful clinical tool in the accurate diagnosis of aMCI and AD. Performance on both short- and long-delay recall trials is helpful in determining if an examinee can retain information adequately over time and recognition trials allow the clinician to better determine if recall deficits are due to poor retrieval or deficits in encoding, as is observed in AD.

Rapid Reference 6.1

CVLT performance in aMCI and AD

Low learning slope (i.e., flat curve)

Low score on Semantic Clustering

Higher recall from Recency section (% Recall from Recency score)

Low score for Short-Delay and Long Delay Free Recall

Minimal improvement on Short-Delay Cued or Long-Delay Cued Recall

Low performance on Yes/No Recognition

Huntington's Disease and CVLT

Unlike with AD, HD affects subcortical regions of the brain and often exhibits executive impairments and a pattern of CVLT performance that is characteristically different from that of aMCI and AD. HD is a genetic neurological disease that results in changes to motor functioning as well as cognitive and behavioral dysfunction. Individuals with HD are frequently referred for cognitive evaluation, including assessment for changes in memory functioning. Although there is far less literature on CVLT performance among individuals with HD compared to those with AD, the literature on HD reveals a distinct pattern in CVLT test performance.

HD typically results in a subcortical dementia. That is, subcortical circuitry involving the basal ganglia and connections to other regions of the brain are affected in HD in a way that affects cognitive abilities. This often results in a dysexecutive learning style. Memory difficulties among individuals with HD typically reflect deficits in retrieval with better performance often detected on recognition measures. Zizak et al. (2005) examined the differential performance of individuals with HD compared to those with Parkinson's disease, specifically comparing retrieval deficits on long-delay free recall and recognition. Individuals with HD were significantly more likely to improve on recognition trials relative to individuals with Parkinson's disease. Moreover, Delis et al. (2005) found no differences between AD and HD patients on basic scores across the CVLT, including immediate recall Trials 1–5, short-delay free and cued recall, and long-delay free and cued recall. However, those with HD displayed much better recall discriminability scores, suggesting they were more accurate in their recall whereas individuals with AD were more likely to include intrusions related to confabulation. Finally, Graves, Holden, Van Etten, et al. (2019) demonstrated that patients with AD compared to those with HD display differential patterns of intrusions on delayed free-recall trials. Specifically, the deficits in encoding associated with AD seem to be predictive of across trial novel intrusions (see Chapter 4), whereas the dysexecutive nature of HD is more associated with across and within trial repeated intrusions. In other words, individuals with HD displayed consistent intrusions across trials whereas individuals with AD exhibited inconsistent, novel intrusions across trials. Other studies have found similar discriminability scores among individuals with HD. In a study comparing those with HD to individuals with multiple sclerosis (MS) and normal controls, individuals with HD exhibited lower scores on long-delay free recall than both normal controls and individuals with multiple sclerosis (MS). Individuals with MS performed similarly to those with HD on Trials 1–5 total learning.

Overall, individuals with HD display difficulties in initial acquisition of the CVLT words across learning trials, difficulties with free recall, but clear improvement on recognition trials. The profile of individuals with HD differs substantially from those with medial temporal lobe abnormalities, such as AD or hippocampal sclerosis. Specifically, the deficits in HD are more characteristic of difficulties with retrieval whereas individuals with medial temporal lobe abnormalities display deficits in encoding. This pattern is sometimes referred to as a subcortical pattern and is also observed among patients with Parkinson's disease, which is discussed next.

Rapid Reference 6.2

CVLT Performance in HD

Low Trials 1–5 Total

Low score for Short-Delay and Long-Delay Free Recall

Clear improvement on Short-Delay Cued or Long-Delay Cued Recall

Improved performance on Yes/No Recognition relative to learning

Parkinson's Disease

Chapter 7 of this text provides a case illustration of interpretation of the CVLT3 for an individual with Parkinson's disease. PD is a progressive movement disorder resulting from deficits in the dopaminergic system of the brain. As the disease progresses, those with PD can display a subcortical pattern of memory and cognitive deficits similar to that seen in individuals with HD and described previously. However, some differences in certain aspects of learning have been observed between HD and PD. Van Etten et al. (2019) compared PD and HD on the CVLT-II and CVLT3 and demonstrated that those with HD displayed lower scores on all recall and recognition discriminability measures. Detailed examination of recall and recognition characteristics can uniquely distinguish HD and PD groups, despite findings that both HD and PD are typically characterized by executive memory deficits due to the frontal-subcortical nature of these diseases. Although differential diagnosis of HD and PD is rarely the referral question for these groups, given that HD is typically diagnosed based on a definitive genetic test, the differences are important to note when interpreting results.

Although utilizing a small sample size, Camicioli et al. (2004) compared individuals with PD to healthy controls on the CVLT-II. Although there were no statistical differences on many CVLT measures, those with PD displayed lower scores on Trials 1–5 total recall, short-delay free recall, and long-delay free recall, and significantly lower scores on short-delay cued recall and long-delay cued recall. Brønnick, Alves, Aarsland, Tysnes, and Larsen (2011) found that individuals with PD displayed lower scores on total learning, short-delay free recall, and long-delay free recall and displayed a lower learning slope than healthy individuals. Importantly, other learning characteristics also differed between groups. Specifically, individuals with PD were less likely to use semantic clustering, consistent with other findings that PD affects executive aspects of performance on CVLT.

CVLT also predicts disease progression in PD, specifically which individuals with PD may eventually develop dementia. Woods and Tröster (2003) examined 118 individuals with PD over a year, 18 of whom converted to PD dementia. Analysis of CVLT performance indicated that the individuals who converted to PD dementia displayed significantly lower scores on Trials 1–5 Total Learning and lower recognition discriminability. A *T* score on Trials 1–5 Total Learning of less than 40 in an individual with PD was highly predictive of developing PD dementia. These findings are supported by additional research indicating that PD is primarily characterized by difficulties with retrieval but normal encoding and recognition. However, once an individual meets criteria for PD dementia, difficulties with encoding and recognition are also present (Higginson, Wheelock, Carroll, & Sigvardt, 2005).

Individuals with PD typically display a pattern of executive deficits, specifically, diminished acquisition and retrieval of information but normal retention (retaining a high percentage of the information learned). Interestingly, individuals with PD often demonstrate improved performance on cued recall, likely due to executive weaknesses in retrieval during free recall despite adequate encoding. Additionally, individuals with PD are less susceptible to false positives and intrusions than those with AD.

Rapid Reference 6.3

CVLT Performance in PD

Low score on Semantic Clustering

Low Trials 1–5 Total

Poor Short-Delay and Long Delay Free Recall

Normal retention (i.e., savings; Trial 5 compared to Short-Delay and Long-Delay Free Recall)

Clear improvement on Short-Delay Cued or Long-Delay Cued Recall

Improved performance on Yes/No Recognition relative to learning

Differentiation of Clinical Groups

Due to the extensive research conducted with the CVLT, performance on the CVLT can help differentiate between different clinical groups. Research described previously shows different patterns in performance among AD, HD, and PD. Additionally, CVLT performance can differentiate among individuals with AD, individuals with Lewy body dementia, and healthy controls. Healthy controls outperform almost all clinical groups on almost all CVLT measures, including long-delay free recall, retention scores, and recognition discriminability. Interestingly, the AD and Lewy body groups were indistinguishable on delayed-free recall intrusions but those with AD were much more likely to provide intrusions during cued-recall tasks. Additionally, individuals with AD were much more likely to perform poorly on recognition tasks relative to individuals with Lewy body dementia (Hamilton et al., 2004). CVLT also differentiates AD and HD. Graves, Holden, Van Etten, et al. (2019) demonstrated that the common deficits in encoding associated with AD are related to across trial novel intrusions, whereas executive weaknesses in HD are more associated with across and within trial repeated intrusions.

In clinical settings, differentiating the cognitive profile of PD from Lewy body dementia can often be difficult. A study by Filoteo et al. (2009) used the CVLT-II to differentiate PD dementia, Lewy body dementia, and healthy control groups. Relative to individuals with PD dementia, those with Lewy body dementia recalled fewer words on learning

Trials 1–4, but similar performance on Trial 5 and similar use of semantic clustering. However, patients with PD were more likely to commit repetition errors on recall trials. Individuals with PD are far more likely to demonstrate perseveration (repetition of words) than individuals with Lewy body dementia. However, the two conditions are indistinguishable on other aspects of learning and recall. This suggests that a differentiation between PD dementia and Lewy body dementia requires evaluation of perseveration and a detailed clinical history.

Memory Change Due to Injury to the Central Nervous System

Traumatic Brain Injury

Understanding the relationship between traumatic brain injury (TBI) and cognitive test performance can be challenging for multiple reasons related to the particular elements of the injury. First, the severity of TBI can range from a mild concussion to severe penetrating injuries and result in varying lengths of loss of consciousness and posttraumatic amnesia. The severity of the TBI is directly correlated with performance on cognitive tests, with greater severity related to lower performance. In addition, TBI can result in diffuse damage to white matter regions of the brain, which can result in changes in focus and concentration, and/or it can result in focal cortical lesions. Depending on the anatomical location of these focal injuries, individuals can have disparate patterns of test performance on the CVLT. Despite the heterogeneity in the clinical symptoms and cognitive profile of individuals with TBI, multiple studies have examined test performance of the CVLT in this population.

One important feature of the literature on CVLT performance in TBI is the analysis of differing test performance across the severity levels of TBI. Vanderploeg, Curtiss, and Belanger (2005) compared healthy individuals to those with mild TBI and a unique additional control group of individuals who had been in motor vehicle accidents but not sustained an injury. The study demonstrated that individuals with mild TBI are more likely to demonstrate proactive interference when comparing Trial 1 to List B. However, there were no differences between the groups on Trials 1–5, long-delay free recall, or recognition hits. The findings suggest that individuals with mild TBI may have difficulties with attention that interferes with learning.

In a longitudinal study of individuals with moderate to severe TBI, Vanderploeg, Donnell, Belanger, and Curtiss (2014) compared performance on CVLT to healthy controls at baseline, 6-month follow-up, and 1-year follow-up. Individuals with TBI had significantly reduced CVLT-II scores across the majority of trials and assessment times. Moreover, at 1 year, those with TBI had significantly lower abilities on short-delay free recall, long-delay free recall, and long-delay cued recall than the healthy controls. Individuals with TBI also displayed a lower learning slope compared to controls at baseline. However, at the 6-month and 12-month follow-up periods, the learning slopes between groups were indistinguishable, illustrating the impact of time from injury on memory functioning. Finally, individuals with TBI were more likely to show proactive interference compared to healthy controls at all time points. In individuals with TBI, although the exact characteristics of learning and memory may fluctuate across time, there is a consistent pattern of deficits in at least some aspect of the CVLT-II across time.

The CVLT-can help predict longitudinal functioning following a TBI. Bercaw, Hanks, Millis, and Gola (2011) demonstrated that a lower CVLT-II performance during a baseline evaluation was predictive of an individual's functional abilities at a 2-year follow-up among patients with moderate to severe TBI. Additionally, Jacobs and Donders (2007) demonstrated that the CVLT-II is able to differentiate controls from those with either mild TBI or moderate to severe TBI. However, it is less accurate at determining the severity of TBI (i.e., severe versus moderate versus mild). Specifically, those with moderate to severe TBI displayed significantly reduced recall abilities and recognition discriminability and more difficulties with total recall discriminability relative to those with milder injuries. However, these groups did not differ on recognition discriminability. Again, individuals with mild injuries were distinguished from healthy controls, with individuals with mild TBI displaying worse recognition discriminability but no difference on total recall discriminability. The total recall discriminability and recognition discriminability were predictive of group membership when comparing controls to TBI groups, with a 66–70% predictive accuracy. Individuals with moderate to severe TBI display significantly lower short-delay free recall, short-delay cued recall, long-delay free recall, long-delay cued recall, recognition discriminability, and recall discriminability relative to healthy controls. Individuals with TBI are also more likely to display intrusions on recall measures. Performance on the CVLT–II allows for the accurate prediction of group membership (controls versus moderate to severe TBI), with indices of discriminability being able to predict group membership 72% of the time and delayed recall measures being able to predict group membership 74% of the time (Donders & Nienhuis, 2007).

The CVLT is a useful clinical tool for understanding verbal learning and memory among individuals with TBI. There is clear evidence from research, however, that performance on the CVLT is likely related to the region of the brain affected by the injury and the severity of the injury. Individuals with moderate to severe injuries display difficulties in initial encoding of information, retrieval after short and long delays, an increased number of intrusions, and reduced discriminability.

Rapid Reference 6.4

CVLT/CVLT-C Performance in TBI

Poor learning observed on Trials 1–5 Total

Poor Short-Delay and Long-Delay Free Recall

Increased number of Total Intrusions

Reduced Discriminability scores

Psychiatric Disorders and Memory

Depression

Clinical literature on depression consistently demonstrates a negative impact of depression on multiple aspects of neurocognitive functioning. This is partly due to the observation that limbic regions of the brain have anatomical overlap with areas responsible for a broad range of executive and memory abilities. As such, it is common for individuals with major depression and other affective conditions to seek cognitive evaluation and depression is frequently a differential diagnosis in dementia evaluation. Fortunately, careful examination of performance on the CVLT can allow a clinician to differentiate dementia from depression.

The profile of CVLT performance among older individuals with depression often takes the form of an executive deficit. Specifically, studies have demonstrated that individuals with major depression display reduced acquisition, reduced learning strategies, and reduced recall, with clear benefit on cueing and recognition tasks (Foldi, Brickman, Schaefer, and Knutelska, 2003; Mesholam-Gately et al., 2012). When comparing unmedicated individuals with major depressive disorder to healthy controls, those with major depression were more likely to use serial clustering than semantic clustering and displayed lower total free recall than their healthy counterparts (Turner, Furey, Drevets, Zarate, & Nugent, 2012). Additionally, performances on independent measures of executive function are predictive of the use of semantic clustering on the CVLT (Elderkin-Thompson, Mintz, Haroon, Lavretsky, & Kumar, 2007). Aspects of the CVLT that can distinguish depression from AD include the percentage of retention scores (savings) and improved performance on cued recall and recognition discriminability. Although depression can show reduced savings and recognition relative to healthy controls, individuals with depression tend to perform better than those with AD.

In addition, examining the serial position of words recalled on learning trials can help distinguish certain clinical groups. For example, individuals with AD are far more likely to recall words from the recency part of the list, echoing back what was heard most recently from the examiner. There is a dissociation between recency and primacy effects between individuals with AD versus depression. Individuals with AD are more likely to display recency effects (Foldi et al., 2003); however, individuals with major depression are more likely to recall words toward the beginning of the list. This primacy effect versus recency effect captured in the CVLT performance provides differentiating information to you in making a clinical determination. Foldi and colleagues also compared healthy controls to AD and depression groups. Although recency and primacy effects distinguished individuals with depression from individuals with AD, those with depression were much less likely to recall items from the middle of the list relative to the healthy control group.

In summary, individuals with depression often display a pattern of memory deficits different from what is observed in AD. That is, depression is marked by diminished acquisition, a tendency to favor primacy relative to recency, and reduced retrieval, but improvement on cued recall and recognition trials.

Rapid Reference 6.5

CVLT performance in depression

Poor learning observed on Trials 1–5 Total
Higher % Primacy relative to % Recency
Reduced retrieval (i.e., low Short-Delay and Long-Delay Free Recall)
Clear improvement on Short-Delay Cued or Long-Delay Cued Recall
Improved performance on Yes/No Recognition relative to learning

Schizophrenia

Understanding the clinical presentation of schizophrenia can be challenging. Individuals may present with more negative symptoms or more positive symptoms and the symptoms can change in severity over time due to medication and other life events. There are also varying degrees of severity and symptoms manifest on a continuum, ranging from mild to severe. As such, it is difficult to find one unitary pattern of memory difficulties in schizophrenia. In fact, research studies have found that some individuals with schizophrenia display a pattern of CVLT performance consistent with a subcortical presentation, including deficits in retrieval, whereas others present with more of a cortical presentation, with deficits in encoding and storage (Brazo, Ilongo, & Dolfus, 2013; Turetsky et al., 2002). Regardless of the pattern, studies consistently demonstrate deficits in verbal learning and memory among individuals with schizophrenia, whether it is an acute presentation or a chronic long-standing presentation (Hill, Beers, Kmiec, & Sweeney, 2004; Hoff, Svetina, Shields, Stewart, & DeLisi, 2005; Rund et al., 2015). Compared to healthy controls, those with schizophrenia display significantly lower performance on Trial 1, Trials 1–5 Total, Short-Delay and Long-Delay Free Recall, and Across-Trial Recall Consistency. Conversely, those with schizophrenia appear to perform similar to their healthy peers on proactive interference (List B versus Trial 1; Hill et al., 2004). There is also evidence that symptom severity is related to CVLT-II outcomes in this patient population, with more severe symptoms being associated with worse performance on Trials 1–5 Total, Short-Delay Free Recall, and Long-Delay Free Recall (Corbett et al., 2018; Stratton, Cobia, Reilly, Brook, & Hanlon, 2018).

The age of onset of initial psychosis may be predictive of cognitive outcomes among those with schizophrenia. In comparing a young age of onset to an older age of onset, those with a younger age of onset were more likely to use intrusions and demonstrate poorer learning strategies, with diminished semantic clustering on learning trials, than those with later onset. This may be why these individuals display lower delayed recall and poor recognition memory (Tuulio-Henriksson, Partonen, Suvisaari, Haukka, & Lönnqvist, 2004).

Rapid Reference 6.6

CVLT performance in schizophrenia

Poor learning observed on Trials 1–5 Total
Poor Short-Delay and Long-Delay Free Recall
Increased number of Total Intrusions
Reduced Discriminability scores

CVLT-C IN CLINICAL POPULATIONS

The CVLT-C was published in 1994 and thousands of studies have been published examining how clinical groups perform on this test. As such, this section on pediatric clinical applications does not cover all possible conditions or provide an exhaustive review of all the literature published with the CVLT-C. Instead, the reviews focus on common conditions seen in clinical settings and how they might perform on this test. This section is divided into those conditions commonly referred in school settings and those from medical settings.

School-Based Assessments

Although schools refer children and adolescents for evaluations for many reasons, the most common are those related to difficulties in learning. These referrals often center around difficulties with learning or attention and often request diagnostic clarity or treatment suggestions. The CVLT-C is an essential tool in evaluating verbal learning and provides insight into the learning strategies and skills utilized by a child. This provides unique insight into subtle diagnostic differences between groups and offers guidance toward possible treatments for learning and memory difficulties.

Attention Deficit/Hyperactivity Disorder

Attention deficit/hyperactivity disorder (ADHD) represents a relatively common developmental condition characterized by either inattention, hyperactivity, or both inattention and hyperactivity. As presented in Chapter 4, multiple aspects of the CVLT are dependent on intact verbal attention and executive skills. As such, the CVLT-C is uniquely sensitive to deficits in memory and learning due to attention and executive difficulties. This implies that special consideration should be made in interpreting the CVLT-C in children and adolescents suspected of having ADHD.

Muir-Broaddus, Rosenstein, Medina, and Soderberg (2002) compared a sample of 65 children with ADHD to the normative sample on several CVLT-C measures. The ADHD group demonstrated significantly lower performance on single trial learning (List A Trial 1 and List B), consistent with interpretation of the performance on the initial learning trial being associated with attention and verbal working memory. Individuals with

ADHD also displayed attenuated learning as measured by Trials 1–5 Total Correct, and reduced retention as indicated by significantly lower short-delay free recall, short-delayed cued-recall and long-delay cued-recall scores than the healthy controls. In the same study, the individuals with ADHD also displayed difficulties with response inhibition with the ADHD group demonstrating significantly more perseverations relative to the normative standardization sample; however, the groups demonstrated similar levels of intrusions on free recall and cued recall trials. Performance on the CVLT-C was significantly correlated to functioning on the Adaptive Behavior Scale (ABS), a parent rating form of a broad range of adaptive behaviors, including subsections specifically related to attention and hyperactivity. Multiple scores on the CVLT-C were significantly correlated with reported behavior, with correlation coefficients ranging from 0.3 to 0.63. In other words, performance on the CVLT-C was correlated with behaviors associated with attention and hyperactivity.

Another study compared children with ADHD to typically developing children, while controlling for any comorbid reading disabilities (Cutting, Koth, Mahone, & Denckla, 2003). This study demonstrated that both groups display similar total learning scores across Trials 1–5. However, children with ADHD displayed lower short-delay free recall and long-delay free recall relative to their healthy counterparts. Children with ADHD also displayed significantly lower levels of recognition relative to controls but the group recognition scores were still in the average range.

In summary, evaluations for ADHD are a common referral from schools. On the CVLT-C, those with ADHD often display low performance on Trial 1 and List B recall due to attenuated verbal working memory. They also display a higher number of repetitions but lower overall scores on Total 1–5 learning, lower Short-Delay Free Recall, Short-Delay Cued Recall, and Long-Delay Cued Recall.

Rapid Reference 6.7

CVLT performance for ADHD

Low single trial performance (i.e., List A Trial 1 and List B)

Low score for Trials 1–5 Total.

Low scores for Short-Delay Free Recall, Short-Delay Cued Recall, and Long-Delay Cued Recall.

Higher number of Repetitions

CVLT-C performance correlates with behavioral deficits in attention and hyperactivity.

Learning Disability

Learning disability (LD) represents a very common referral question from school settings. There are multiple types of learning disabilities and an individual child may present with more than one type. In addition, there are frequent comorbidities with a LD, such as ADHD. Therefore, it is important to understand the child's family history, educational history, and specific learning difficulties before the evaluation. It is also important to understand the criteria used within a school district or state to define LD as there is not a uniform diagnostic criteria. One specific type of LD is dyslexia. It is important to note that the definition of dyslexia has changed over the lifetime of the CVLT-C and care needs to be taken when selecting studies to help guide your knowledge of how children with dyslexia and other learning disorders perform. Most studies utilizing the CVLT-C, due to the age of the instrument, define dyslexia as reading below grade level, with a one standard deviation discrepancy between reading ability and intelligence. Reading deficits in dyslexia cannot be better accounted for by other neurological or medical conditions, psychiatric disturbance, or quality of education (including participation in the learning environment).

Research indicates that children with dyslexia display poor encoding on learning trials of the CVLT-C but exhibit relatively normal retention and retrieval abilities. They also display normal scores on proactive (List B vs. Trial 1) and retroactive interference measures (Short-Delay Free Recall vs. Trial 5), as well as normal levels of intrusions. However, relative to healthy controls, children with dyslexia recall fewer words from the middle of the list, possibly due to poor encoding and difficulties with semantic clustering (Kramer, Knee, & Delis, 2000). It is important to note that overall cognitive ability may account for some of these differences; Kibby (2009) found that children with dyslexia perform similar to healthy controls when verbal intelligence is controlled for in the comparisons. General verbal abilities likely play a critical role in the assessment of learning disorders, as children with specific language impairment display attenuated free recall on learning trials of the CVLT-C relative to healthy controls (Duinmeijer, de Jong, & Scheper, 2012). Given the potential of multiple difficulties within a child, it is important to evaluate all aspects of language and learning functioning when assessing for learning difficulties.

Fisher and DeLuca (1997) directly compared children and adults with a nonverbal LD to children and adults with a verbal LD. The combined child and adult sample was administered the CVLT-C for children and the CVLT for adults. The two LD groups differed significantly in serial versus semantic clustering. Specifically, those with nonverbal LD were far more likely to use serial clustering than semantic clustering, with average performance for serial clustering but impaired semantic clustering. Conversely, those with a verbal LD were more likely to use semantic clustering, but both serial and semantic clustering scores were in the normal (average) range for this group.

In summary, although LD is a common referral question, it is important to know that the cognitive pattern in this patient group is quite heterogeneous. Although CVLT-C is not often used in diagnosing learning disabilities, it is needed to evaluate the impact of various learning differences and to provide guidance on specific processes that may be important to address in intervention planning. CVLT-C performance is correlated with verbal abilities. Those with LD often show attenuated encoding as manifest in poor learning on Trials 1–5. However, studies suggest that LD can display normal Short-Delay and Long-Delay Free Recall, normal Proactive and Retroactive Interference, and normal levels of intrusions.

Rapid Reference 6.8

CVLT performance for learning disability

Mixed findings—Performances are correlated with verbal abilities (many normal scores when verbal abilities are statistically controlled for)

Poor encoding (i.e., poor learning observed on Trials 1–5 Total)

Normal retention (i.e., normal Short-Delay and Long-Delay Free Recall)

Normal Proactive and Retroactive Interference

Normal levels of Intrusions

Those with dyslexia display lower % Middle scores

Healthcare-Based Assessments

Referrals from healthcare settings involve a plethora of disorders, both genetic and acquired. Evaluations for medically complex cases involving children often involve concerns about the impact of a condition or a treatment on a child or adolescent's cognitive functioning, including learning and memory. For these cases, complete medical, family, educational, and social histories are key to understanding and interpreting CVLT-C and other test results.

Down Syndrome

Down syndrome (DS) is a genetic condition that commonly relates to cognitive, learning, adaptive, and behavior difficulties. In fact, DS is the most common cause of intellectual disability and individuals with DS are frequently referred for cognitive evaluations (Godfrey & Lee, 2018). Although the diagnosis of intellectual disability may be part of the evaluation, learning strengths and weaknesses, and guidance on appropriate teaching strategies to accommodate the child's unique learning abilities are often the most important outcome of an evaluation. As such, much work has been done to understand the cognitive profile of those with DS, including examination of learning and memory using the CVLT-C. Nichols et al. (2004) examined the distinct CVLT-C profiles of multiple clinical groups, including children with Williams syndrome, DS, language impairment, and perinatal focal brain injuries. These children were compared to healthy controls on multiple aspects of the CVLT-C. Children with DS perform significantly worse on all aspects of the CVLT-C relative to typically developing children. Children with DS also exhibit more intrusions on recall trials and more false positives on recognition trials. In comparison to other clinical groups, children with DS obtain the lowest scores for List A Trial 1 and List B recall. They also demonstrate some of the highest intrusion rates compared to the other clinical groups. Finally, individuals with DS displayed greater difficulties with recognition discriminability relative to typically developing healthy controls

(Nichols et al., 2004). Taken together, those with DS often display impairments in learning, recall, discriminability, and a high number of intrusions.

Rapid Reference 6.9

CVLT performance for Down syndrome

Reduced scores are correlated with language functioning

Lower scores on List A Trial 1, List A Trial 5, List B, Short-Delay Free Recall, Long-Delay Free Recall

Higher occurrence of Total Intrusions

Poor Discriminability scores

Pediatric Traumatic Brain Injury

Similar to the discussion on TBI in adults, children with TBI exhibit different patterns on the CVLT-C based on the severity and location of the injury, as well as time since injury. A case illustration of pediatric mild TBI is presented in Chapter 4. In general, the results described in the adult TBI review also apply to pediatric TBI. Yeates, Blumenstein, Patterson, and Delis (1995) examined the performance on the CVLT-C across different severity levels of pediatric TBI. Children with mild to moderate injuries display similar learning and similar recognition abilities to individuals without a TBI history. However, those with mild to moderate injuries display impairments in long-delay free recall relative to healthy controls. Performance was significantly worse in children with severe injuries. Specifically, children with severe TBI displayed lower Trials 1–5 Total scores and deficits in long-delay free recall. Children with severe TBI also demonstrated more errors with recognition memory and were more vulnerable to intrusions on recall tasks. Greater injury severity in pediatric TBI is also associated with a lower learning slope observed on Trials 1–5. Relative to more mild injuries, children with more severe injuries displayed incrementally lower learning slopes and plateaued more quickly than individuals with mild to moderate injuries (Warschausky, Kay, Chi, & Donders, 2005).

Mottram and Donders (2006) examined memory performance in 175 children with various severities of TBI. They found that children with the worst CVLT-C performance also presented with a longer length of coma at the time of injury. They also demonstrated that CVLT-C performance in children with TBI was correlated with processing speed, which is consistent with other literature indicating that executive abilities are necessary for adequate performance on this test (Delis, Cullum, Butters, Cairns, & Prifitera, 1988; Delis, Freeland, Kramer, & Kaplan, 1988). Studies of pediatric TBI have also used the CVLT to examine the different process scores on the CVLT-C. Donders and Minnema (2004) demonstrated that children with TBI are far more likely than children in the standardization sample to exhibit proactive interference. In fact, children with anterior lesions were three times more likely to exhibit proactive interference compared to other children with TBI not associated with frontal lesions.

Cancer and Cancer Treatment

Cancer is a terrifying diagnosis for children and families and a psychologist is often brought in to assess a family's concerns around cognitive difficulties related to both the disease and the impact of treatment. Understanding the cognitive impact of pediatric brain cancer and cancer treatment is difficult due to the heterogeneity of the disease process and the broad range of treatment procedures. Assessing children with cancer requires significant knowledge and training in working with this population and their families, understanding the disease process and how it affects cognitive and psychological functioning and understanding the interaction of medicine, medical treatments, and other factors. However, because the CVLT-C is commonly used in assessments of children with cancer, a few studies are reviewed here to provide insight into its use in this population.

A 9-year longitudinal study on memory abilities among children with pediatric low-grade gliomas who were treated with whole-brain radiation found that whole-brain radiation had a negative impact on total learning, short-delay free recall, and long-delay free-recall scores, with significant declines across the study time frame. There were also detrimental effects observed in learning characteristics, such as diminished use of semantic clustering and poor recall discriminability. Although this study demonstrated that individuals treated with radiation continue to experience cognitive difficulties long after treatment, they also found that the magnitude of change was negatively associated with the dose of radiation targeted toward hippocampal regions. Specifically, greater hippocampal dose was related to greater cognitive decline (Acharya et al., 2019). Alternately, Di Pinto, Conklin, Li, and Merchant (2012) evaluated children who had either low-grade gliomas or craniopharyngioma and who received chemotherapy and radiation therapy, 5 years after they ended treatment. In this study, CVLT-C performance was average at baseline and across a 5-year span for children with low-grade gliomas, and children with craniopharyngioma exhibited average performance at baseline and statistical improvement at the 5-year follow-up. No changes in learning and memory abilities due to radiation therapy were observed. However, other secondary factors appeared to moderate scores on CVLT-C. For example, the presence of hydrocephalus in the craniopharyngioma group predicted worse verbal learning at baseline but not at the 5-year mark. Shunting in this group also related to worse CVLT-C total learning scores at the 5-year mark. Among those with low-grade glioma, shunt insertion and preradiation chemotherapy predicted worse abilities in CVLT-C verbal learning at the 5-year mark. Complications with treatment are associated with worse outcomes among these cancer populations. This illustrates the need for a complete medical history in interpreting results on CVLT-C and other measures.

Di Pinto, Conklin, Li, Xiong, and Merchant (2010) also studied localized ependymoma in a sample of 71 children and examined cognitive outcomes with the CVLT-C. Cognitive abilities were measured before conformal radiation therapy, at 6 months post radiation therapy, and then annually for a total of 5 years. The entire patient group performed in the average range at baseline and there was a trend toward improved CVLT-C performance at the 5-year mark following treatment. Similar to the prior study, a more complicated clinical history was related to poorer outcomes among younger children.

Individuals with multiple surgeries for tumor resection who also required shunting of the cerebrospinal fluid displayed worse CVLT-C performance at baseline and a slower recovery than their older counterparts. However, these negative outcomes at baseline diminished over time and no differences were observed at the 5-year mark.

In summary, there are mixed findings in the literature as to memory functioning in children with cancer. There is evidence of relatively good outcomes, with some studies demonstrating that a complicated clinical course can also impact CVLT-C outcomes. However, it should be stressed that pediatric cancer and cancer treatment are complicated and heterogeneous in nature. There are many studies demonstrating deficits in other cognitive domains, including diminished executive functioning, reduced attention and processing speed, and other focal cognitive deficits depending on the anatomical region involved. A review of all aspects of cognitive functioning in this patient group is beyond the scope of this chapter and readers are encouraged to pursue additional literature on general cognitive functioning in pediatric cancer as needed.

Rapid Reference 6.10

CVLT performance for pediatric cancer

Mixed findings—Relatively good outcomes

Poor outcomes for those with a more complicated clinical course

TEST YOURSELF

1. **Which of the following is NOT true of the typical pattern of CVLT performance in those with AD?**
   (a) A flat learning curve (low Learning Slope score).
   (b) A tendency to recall words from the beginning of the list.
   (c) Poor Semantic Clustering.
   (d) Impaired Cued Recall.
2. **Higher rates of intrusions are expected in AD.**
   True or False
3. **The memory profile of Huntington's disease typically includes which of the following?**
   (a) Low Trials 1–5 Total.
   (b) Better performance with Cued Recall and Yes/No Recognition.
   (c) Reduced Semantic Clustering.
   (d) All of the above.

4. **Research on the CVLT in TBI populations has taught us that ____.**
   (a) Performance is related to injury severity.
   (b) Mild TBI patients perform the same as moderate TBI patients.
   (c) Posterior lesions are associated with worse outcomes.
   (d) CVLT performance does not predict functional abilities.
5. **What is a distinguishing feature of CVLT performance in depression?**
   (a) Those with depression display an amnestic pattern of testing, with very low recall and recognition.
   (b) Although memory may be impaired, they typically display better semantic clustering than serial clustering.
   (c) They often benefit from cued recall and Yes/No recognition trials.
   (d) They appear to have a similar pattern to AD but not Lewy body dementia.
6. **Studies of CVLT-C performances demonstrate that outcomes are correlated with verbal abilities.**
   True or False

Answers: 1. b, 2. True, 3. d, 4. a, 5. c, 6. True

Seven

ILLUSTRATIVE CASE REPORTS

This chapter presents multiple illustrative case reports of specific patient populations and their performance on the California Verbal Learning Test (CVLT). The initial case provides a baseline performance though an individual demonstrating typical memory performance as assessed by the CVLT3. Three additional adult cases are then presented along with one pediatric case, each selected to demonstrate specific aspects of performance on one or more versions of the CVLT. These cases provide a new user with concrete examples of the application of the CVLT measures in a clinical case and a means of understanding how data might be interpreted. More detailed information on the interpretation of the CVLT, including interpretation of individual scores, is discussed in Chapter 4.

CASE 1 (S.R.)—TYPICAL MEMORY

S. R. is a 45-year-old right-handed Caucasian female with 16 years of education. She is a native English speaker. She was referred for a neuropsychological evaluation due to ongoing cognitive difficulties following a motor vehicle accident sustained 1 year prior to evaluation. Brain imaging was notable for an incidental finding of an old small infarct, which was thought to be unrelated to her accident. Her cognitive concerns included reduced attention and concentration, difficulties with planning and organizing at work, and difficulties with problem-solving. She also reported specific memory concerns, including forgetting work-related tasks and trouble recalling recent events. S. R. expressed concern that her memory difficulties are having a significant impact on her quality of life, including possible difficulties with completing her job, which was placing her employment at risk. Historically, there were no additional neurological factors. She did endorse mild depression over the last 3 years and indicated that mood symptoms have worsened since her motor vehicle accident. There was no relevant family medical history. There was no pending litigation related to her injury. Based on her concerns, a comprehensive neuropsychological assessment was performed, including the CVLT3.

The multiple scores presented in Table 7.1 provide an overview of S.R.'s memory performance on CVLT. As recommended in Chapter 4, interpretation begins with the primary scores.

1. Trial 1 Total Correct: S. R. recalled 7 items on Trial 1, a scaled score of 11, which is in the average range.
2. Trials 1–5 Total Correct: She freely recalled 63 total items across learning trials, a scaled score of 115, which is one standard deviation above the mean.
3. Trial B Total Correct: She recalled 9 items from List B, a scaled score of 15, which is one standard deviation above the mean.
4. Recall Items: All recall items, including short-delay free, short-delay cued, long-delay free, and long-delay cued, were between 13 and 14 words, with scaled scores ranging from 12 to 13 (average to high average).
5. Yes/No recognition: She recognized 15 of the 16 List A words, suggesting normal recognition of information.
6. Forced-Choice recognition: She correctly selected every List A word for 100% recognition, suggesting appropriate effort on the test or normal performance validity.

The CVLT3 was administered as part of a comprehensive battery that allows interpretation of scores within the context of her other cognitive abilities. S. R. performed within an average to above average range on all other measures of attention, executive function, language, and visual-spatial skills. Therefore, her memory scores align with her other cognitive ability scores.

From the primary scores alone, S. R. exhibits intact memory abilities. However, further analysis of learning characteristics provides a greater look at her learning and memory characteristics. For example, S. R. was more likely to use semantic clustering than serial clustering, which suggests intact executive skills. Recall from primacy, middle, or recency sections of the list were relatively evenly spaced, with 44% of her recall coming from the middle of the list. All standard scores for primacy, middle, and recency were within an average range. She also displayed an average learning slope, acquiring an average of 1.9 words across each trial. Finally, she responded with four intrusions across the trials, which is in the average range.

S. R. exhibited typical learning and memory ability across all trials of the CVLT3. Her performance was consistent with her other cognitive performances and her learning style suggests good executive skills. At this point in time, S. R. is not demonstrating any clear deficits and is performing at a level consistent with her peers. Although, one caveat to this conclusion is that there was no preexisting cognitive data to confirm that she did not decline from a previously higher level of functioning. Clinicians should always take caution in interpreting data, even when data appear normal.

CASE 2 (D. B.)—PROBABLE ALZHEIMER'S DISEASE

D. B. is a 77-year-old, left-handed female with 12-years of education. She is of mixed ethnic heritage (Brazilian-Italian) and is a fluent English speaker. She was referred for a 2-year follow-up comprehensive neuropsychological evaluation by her primary care provider. At her baseline evaluation, D. B. was assessed using the CVLT-II, along with a battery of

Table 7.1 CVLT3 Performance for S. R.

Variable	Raw score	Standard score
Trial 1 Total Correct	7	11
Trial 5 Total Correct	15	13
Trial 1–5 Total Correct	63	115 (SS)
Total Learning Slope Trials 1–5	1.9	12
Semantic Clustering	5.1	15
Serial Clustering Forward	−0.3	6
Percent Recall Primacy	31%	11
Percent Recall Middle	44%	9
Percent Recall Recency	26%	10
Trial B Total Correct	9	15
Short–Delayed Free-Recall Correct	13	12
Short–Delayed Cued-Recall Correct	14	13
Long–Delay Free-Recall Correct	14	12
Long–Delayed Cued-Recall Correct	14	12
Total Free-Recall Intrusions	2	10
Total Cued-Recall Intrusions	2	8
Total Intrusions (All Recall Trials, All Types)	4	9
Total Repetitions (All Recall Trials)	4	11
Long-Delay Yes/No Recognition Hits	15/16	9
Long-Delay Yes/No Recognition False Positives	1	10
Long-Delay Yes/No Recognition Total Response Bias	0.2	12
Long-Delay Yes/No Total Recognition Discriminability	3.4	10
Long-Delay Forced-Choice Recognition Accuracy	16/16	100%

Note: Standard scores are a mean of 10 and a standard deviation of 3. SS = Index Score, with a mean of 100 and a standard deviation of 15.

other tests. She was initially diagnosed as having mild cognitive impairment, amnestic subtype (MCI-amnestic). At this 2-year follow-up, her family expressed concern about additional cognitive declines. She originally presented to her primary care provider with family members who expressed concern that D. B. was displaying difficulties with her memory over the previous 3–4 years. She is now approximately 6 years from the onset of her reported memory decline. D. B. largely denied any concerns about her cognitive abilities and reported feeling fine. When pressed further with specific examples of memory difficulties, she again denied having any major problems and reported feeling that she was the same as her healthy peers. Her family members, in contrast, provided specific examples of memory difficulties, including rapidly forgetting recent information, often repeating herself, requiring information to be repeated frequently, forgetting upcoming events, and displaying intermittent confusion. There was also a report of some difficulties with word finding. D. B. was also mildly paranoid and expressed fear that people were stealing things from her house. D. B. had a positive family history of dementia; specifically, her father passed away in his mid-80s from dementia of unknown etiology. She also had a paternal aunt diagnosed with dementia of the Alzheimer's type in her mid-70s. D. B.'s brother died at the age of 82 after having dementia of unclear etiology for approximately 5 years. D. B. and her family denied any prior neurological or psychiatric history that might contribute to her current difficulties.

Despite reporting that she was not concerned about her cognition, D. B. consented to engage in the neuropsychological evaluation. The test battery included a broad range of measures, although the total testing time was truncated in order to minimize fatigue and testing frustration. Although the CVLT3 is the most recent publication, the CVLT-II was administered to allow direct comparison of the current results to the previous assessment results. Her scores on the CVLT-II are listed in Table 7.2.

The primary scores describe D. B.'s basic learning and memory abilities as measured on the CVLT-II.

1. Trial 1 Total Correct: D. B. recalled five words on Trial 1. This was a *z*-score of −0.5, which is in the average range. This was similar to her working memory capacity as measured on a digit span task.
2. Trials 1–5 Total Correct: She obtained a total learning score of 25 items across learning trials. This is a *T* score of 32, which is 1.75 standard deviations below the mean or at the fourth percentile and suggests moderate difficulties with learning across trials.
3. List B Total Correct: She recalled four words on this distractor list, which was 0.5 standard deviations below the mean, which is in the average range and similar to her performance on Trial 1 of List A.
4. Recall Items
   a. Short-Delay Free Recall: Immediately after List B, D. B. displayed poor recall and retention of List A, recalling only one item. This is two standard deviations below the mean for her age.
   b. Short-Delay Cued Recall: For most healthy examinees, cued-recall trials aid in retrieval. In this case, she recalled three total items with the aid of cues. However, this was still 2.5 standard deviations below the mean for age, which is impaired and suggests that cueing is not helping her recall information. This can provide the clinician important information about whether the examinee has adequate encoding.
   c. Long-Delay Free Recall: After a longer delay, we see that D. B. failed to recall any items from the list. However, this level of impairment could be due to poor executive skills and self-initiated retrieval. As such, the cued-recall trial becomes very important to distinguish whether the 0 item recall was because of poor encoding or poor retrieval.
   d. Long-Delay Cued Recall: Even with cues, D. B. was unable to recall any items. This suggests poor encoding, with rapid forgetting of information.
      i. In summary, all recall items were attenuated, falling 2–2.5 standard deviations below the mean, suggesting impaired recall. Notably, she did not appear

Table 7.2 CVLT-II Performance for D. B. – Probable Alzheimer's

Variable	Raw score	Standard score
Trial 1 Total Correct	5	−0.5
Trial 5 Total Correct	5	−2.5
Trial 1–5 Total Correct	25	32 (*T* score)
Total Learning Slope Trials 1–5	0.2	−2.5
Semantic Clustering	−0.6	−1
Serial Clustering Forward	1.3	1.5
Percent Recall Primacy	8%	−3
Percent Recall Middle	36%	−1
Percent Recall Recency	56%	3
Trial B Total Correct	4	−0.5
List B versus Trial 1 of List A	−20%	0
Short-Delayed Free-Recall Correct	1	−2
Short-Delayed Cued-Recall Correct	3	−2.5
Long-Delay Free-Recall Correct	0	−2.5
Long-Delayed Cued-Recall Correct	0	−2.5
Total Free-Recall Intrusions	2	0
Total Cued-Recall Intrusions	9	2
Total Intrusions (All Recall Trials, All Types)	11	1
Total Repetitions (All Recall Trials)	3	0
Long-Delay Yes/No Recognition Hits	0	−5
Long-Delay Yes/No Recognition False Positives	1	−0.5
Long-Delay Yes/No Recognition Total Response Bias	1.9	5
Long-Delay Yes/No Total Recognition Discriminability	0	−3.5
Long-Delay Yes/No Source Recognition Discriminability	0	−3.5
Long-Delay Yes/No Novel Recognition Discriminability	−0.3	−4

to benefit from cued recall during short delay or long delay. She recalled no words on either long-delay free recall or long-delay cued recall, which is often observed in medial temporal lobe dysfunction, such as Alzheimer's disease.

D. B. displayed adequate auditory working memory but difficulties with the acquisition of verbal information over time and significant difficulty with recalling information either over a short-delay or long-delay interval. Examining the learning and memory characteristics of her performance provided additional information about differential diagnosis.

Individuals with Alzheimer's disease often show a differential pattern for semantic clustering versus serial clustering. D. B. exhibited this pattern; she was less likely to use semantic clustering and more likely to use serial clustering. This suggests that she was unable to use executive strategies to organize words into semantic groupings, instead repeating the words in the same order in which they were read. She also exhibited a strong recency effect on learning trials; 56% of the words she provided on learning trials were from the recency section of the list whereas only 8% came from the primacy section. This suggests she may simply be echoing the most recent thing she heard. The lack of recall from primacy suggests that she is not converting words from the beginning of the list into long-term memory. D. B.'s total learning slope was −2.5 standard deviations below the mean, suggesting a very flat learning curve. In fact, she recalled 5, 4, 5, 6, and 5 across the five learning trials, respectively. The CVLT is rarely used in isolation to make a diagnosis and D. B. was administered CVLT-II within a wider battery and known history. Her previous CVLT performance was described as amnestic, suggesting rapid forgetting and minimal to no benefit from a recognition format. Her current performance is consistent with this previous analysis. When all the information was considered in conjunction with other test performances and clinical history, the clinician made a diagnosis of probable Alzheimer's disease.

CASE 3 (J. L.)—PARKINSON'S DISEASE

J. L. is a 63-year-old Native American female with 16 years of education. J. L. was referred by a multidisciplinary team from neurology and neurosurgery for a comprehensive neuropsychological examination related to treatment options for Parkinson's disease (PD). J. L. was being considered for deep brain stimulation (DBS) surgery after 7 years of motor symptoms from PD. DBS is a surgical procedure in which an electrode is implanted into a specific area of the basal ganglia of the brain, which can drastically reduce motor symptoms and improve functioning and quality of life. However, dementia is a contraindication for DBS surgery and those with Parkinson's disease are frequently referred for cognitive evaluation prior to surgery.

Her motor symptoms began approximately 7 years prior to the neuropsychological consultation. In addition to her motor symptoms, she displayed many of the signs and symptoms common to PD, including a soft voice (hypophonia), blank facial expression (masked facies), slow verbal responses and slow mental processing (bradyphrenia), and a shuffled-stooped gait. She endorsed cognitive difficulties, including slowed processing, difficulties tracking conversations, trouble multitasking and problem-solving, and mild memory difficulties. She was administered a comprehensive neuropsychological assessment which included the CVLT3. Her CVLT3 results are described in Table 7.3.

The results of the CVLT3 show that J. L. performed in the average range for most primary measures of memory. Individuals with PD typically display a pattern of executive deficits. Specifically, individuals with PD often display diminished acquisition and retrieval of information but often show fairly normal savings (retaining a high percentage of the information learned). J. L.'s learning and recall scores were in the average range, with a standard score of 92 on Trials 1–5 and scaled scores of 8 on short- and long-delay recall trials. Interestingly, individuals with PD often demonstrate improved performance on cued recall, likely due to executive weaknesses in spontaneous self-derived free recall

Table 7.3 CVLT3 Performance for J. L.

Variable	Raw score	Standard score
Trial 1 Total Correct	5	10
Trial 5 Total Correct	9	8
Trial 1–5 Total Correct	43	92 (SS)
Total Learning Slope Trials 1–5	0.9	8
Semantic Clustering	−0.7	6
Serial Clustering Forward	1	13
Percent Recall Primacy	51%	18
Percent Recall Middle	38%	9
Percent Recall Recency	11%	2
Trial B Total Correct	5	11
Short-Delay Free-Recall Correct	7	8
Short-Delay Cued-Recall Correct	12	11
Long-Delay Free-Recall Correct	8	8
Long-Delay Cued-Recall Correct	12	11
Total Free-Recall Intrusions	0	13
Total Cued-Recall Intrusions	0	13
Total Intrusions (All Recall Trials, All Types)	0	14
Total Repetitions (All Recall Trials)	0	15
Long-Delay Yes/No Recognition Hits	15	10
Long-Delay Yes/No Recognition False Positives	0	14
Long-Delay Yes/No Recognition Total Response Bias	0.3	12
Long-Delay Forced-Choice Recognition Accuracy	16/16	100%

Note: Standard scores are a mean of 10 and a standard deviation of 3. SS = Index Score, with a mean of 100 and a standard deviation of 15.

despite adequate encoding. This is observed in J. L.'s CVLT3 performance. The short-delay and long-delay cued-recall scaled scores are each 11; the cued-recall scores are one standard deviation higher than free-recall scores. This difference suggests that J. L. benefited from cueing and that she may have the retrieval difficulties commonly observed in PD. Similarly, she recognized 15 out of the 16 words on Yes/No recognition, obtaining an average scaled score of 10. Individuals with PD are less susceptible to false positives and intrusions than those with Alzheimer's disease or Korsakoff's syndrome and J. L. did not demonstrate any false positives on recognition trials. Examination of her secondary scores revealed that she was less likely to use executive learning strategies. Specifically, semantic clustering was a scaled score of 6, which is 1.33 standard deviations below the mean. She appeared to favor the more direct approach of serial clustering, which was a scaled score of 13, or one standard deviation above the mean.

J. L. went on to display fairly normal functioning on other memory and language tests. However, she did display mildly reduced visual-spatial skills and mildly to moderately reduced processing speed and executive functioning. Her overall pattern of cognitive abilities was similar to other PD cases. There were no major impairments that would preclude her from DBS candidacy and she was scheduled for surgery shortly after neuropsychological testing.

CASE 4 (N.C.)—MULTIPLE SCLEROSIS

Individuals with multiple sclerosis (MS) are often referred for a comprehensive neuropsychological assessment for the purposes of tracking cognitive symptoms over time and determination of disability status. N. C. is a 42-year-old Hispanic female with 14 years of education. She was diagnosed with MS approximately 8 years prior to the evaluation, but she had not been previously assessed by neuropsychology. She presented for testing due to reported changes in cognition and recent termination from her job due to cognitive errors. She was actively pursuing a disability application through the state. She presented with multiple cognitive concerns, including short-term memory declines, difficulties with planning and organizing, slowed processing, word-finding difficulties, and deficits in problem-solving. However, she also presented with additional health concerns that can have a negative impact on cognition. Specifically, she endorsed a moderate degree of chronic nerve pain. Chronic pain can interfere with cognitive performance in the areas of attention and executive functioning. Additionally, N. C. reported receiving only 4 hr of sleep at night; she indicated that she has severe obstructive sleep apnea for which she is not treated. This level of sleep disturbance, as well as sleep apnea, can also interfere with cognitive functioning. An MRI of her brain revealed a significant number of MS-related lesions but her clinical history of pain and poor sleep must also be taken into account when interpreting her test results. She was administered the CVLT3 as part of a comprehensive neuropsychological evaluation. Her results are reported in Table 7.4.

N. C.'s primary scores describe her level of learning and memory ability.

1. Trial 1 Total Correct: N. C. recalled three items on Trial 1, which was a scaled score of 4 or two standard deviations below the mean (second percentile). This suggests difficulties with auditory attention and working memory. However, she performed better on other auditory working memory tests, suggesting the initial trial may have been anxiety-provoking (see Chapter 4).
2. Trials 1–5 Total Correct: She freely recalled 34 total items across learning trials, which is a scaled score of 81 or approximately 1.3 standard deviations below the mean and in the low average range. This suggests some mild difficulties with learning.
3. List B Total Correct: She recalled six items from List B, which was a scaled score of 11 (average). The contrast in Trial 1 of List A and the better performance for List B again supports the idea that the initial exposure to the list was overwhelming and not necessarily indicative of verbal attention and working memory problems.
4. Recall Items
   a. On short-delay free recall, she recalled six items, a scaled score of 6, suggesting a mild weakness with recall after an interference trial.

Table 7.4 CVLT3 Performance for N. C. (Multiple Sclerosis)

Variable	Raw score	Standard score
Trial 1 Correct	3	4
Trial 5 Correct	10	7
Trial 1–5 Correct	34	81 (SS)
Total Learning Slope Trials 1–5	1.6	11
Semantic Clustering	0.1	8
Serial Clustering Forward	1.4	13
Percent Recall Primacy	26%	9
Percent Recall Middle	39%	8
Percent Recall Recency	34%	13
Trial B Correct	6	11
Short-Delay Free-Recall Correct	6	6
Short-Delay Cued-Recall Correct	8	7
Long-Delay Free-Recall Correct	6	5
Long-Delay Cued-Recall Correct	8	7
Total Free-Recall Intrusions	2	10
Total Cued-Recall Intrusions	2	8
Total Intrusions (All Recall Trials, All Types)	1	12
Total Repetitions (All Recall Trials)	4	11
Long-Delay Yes/No Recognition Hits	13	6
Long-Delay Yes/No Recognition False Positives	0	13
Long-Delay Yes/No Recognition Total Response Bias	0.2	12
Long-Delay Forced-Choice Recognition Accuracy	16/16	100%

Note: Standard scores are a mean of 10 and a standard deviation of 3. SS = Index Score, with a mean of 100 and a standard deviation of 15.

b. On short-delay cued recall, she recalled eight words, two additional words were recalled with cueing. The scaled score of 7 is in the low average range and suggests a modest benefit from cueing.
c. On long-delay free recall, she recalled six words (60% savings compared to Trial 5 of 10 items). This corresponds to a scaled score of 5, which is around 1.66 standard deviations below the mean and indicates performance in the borderline range. This free-recall performance indicates that N. C. has diminished retrieval and mild to moderate difficulties in verbal memory recall following the passage of time.
d. On long-delay cued recall, she again demonstrated modest improvements, with two additional items recalled and a scaled score in the low average range (7).

5. Yes/No recognition: N. C. recognized 13 of the 16 List A words, a scaled score of 6. This suggests that she encoded more words than she freely recalled but her performance was lower than expected in relation to her same age peers.

6. Given N. C.'s potential secondary gain in relation to her pending disability claim, it is important to review the forced-choice recognition score to evaluate performance validity. She obtained a perfect score on forced-choice recognition, recognizing all 16 of the List A words. This is consistent with normal scores on additional performance validity scores and suggests a valid assessment of her abilities.

These primary scores suggest that N. C. is having difficulties in both acquisition and recall of verbal content. She does display a normal learning curve, acquiring 1–2 words per trial, but low total learning. She also benefits from cues and has no difficulties distinguishing targets from nontargets on Yes/No recognition. She retained 60% of learned material over time. Together, these data indicate she is encoding more information than she can freely recall. Further analysis of a few process scores reveals more evidence of an executive weakness her test performance. Specifically, semantic clustering was a scaled score of 8 and serial clustering was a scaled score of 13. This is a standard score difference of 1.66 standard deviations and indicates that she is not using executive strategies to learn the list of words. Although additional data from testing are not presented in Table 7.4, N. C. was also administered a contextual verbal memory test made up of short stories, and her performance on this verbal memory test was much stronger relative to the CVLT. The CVLT typically requires more executive skill than verbal tests presented as short stories as there is not a context around the information to be recalled in CVLT. Many examinees with executive difficulties will display more difficulties recalling word lists than verbal prose, similar to the pattern seen for N. C. She had the most difficulty on executive tests and executive aspects of additional testing areas, a pattern commonly observed in individuals with MS. In interpreting the results, it is important to consider the additional clinical factors that could negatively affect performance, namely her chronic pain and sleep disorder. These factors were central to the treatment recommendations for N. C.

In summary, individuals with MS often display attenuated memory performance in a pattern suggesting some executive weaknesses, with better encoding than free recall, and improvement with recognition format. In N. C.'s case, additional secondary factors should also be considered as possible contributors to memory and cognitive deficits, namely chronic pain and sleep disorder.

CASE 5 (G. G.)—MILD TRAUMATIC BRAIN INJURY: PEDIATRIC CASE

The prevalence of traumatic brain injury (TBI) is high in pediatric groups with the majority of TBI cases being mild in severity. As such, mild TBI (mTBI) is a common reason for referral for cognitive assessment. G. G. is a 15-year-old African-American female who sustained an mTBI resulting from a sport-related injury. She was referred for an evaluation several months after the injury due to ongoing cognitive difficulties. She was historically an average to above average student, typically obtaining a "B" average in school. However, she reported that she has been struggling with completing coursework, managing multiple class demands, and attending to lectures since her injury. There were no additional secondary neurological or psychiatric factors present that are known to impact testing. G. G. was administered the CVLT-C as part of a larger neuropsychological evaluation; results are shown in Table 7.5.

Table 7.5 CVLT-C Performance for G. G.

Measure	Raw score	*T* score
List A Total Trials 1–5	35	26
Measure	Raw score	*z*-score
List A Trial 1 Free Recall	3	−2.5
List A Trial 5 Free Recall	10	−1.5
List B Free Recall	3	−2.0
List A Short-Delay Free Recall	10	−0.5
List A Short-Delay Cued Recall	9	−1.0
List A Long-Delay Free Recall	7	−1.5
List A Long-Delay Cued Recall	9	−1.0
Semantic Cluster Ratio	1.4	0.0
Serial Cluster Ratio	2.4	0.0
Percent Primacy Recall	35	1.5
Percent Middle Recall	42	0.0
Percent Recency Recall	27	0.0
Learning Slope	1.4	0.0
Recall Consistency	87	0.5
Response Bias	0	0.0
Correct Recognition Hits	11	−0.5
False Positives (*)	0	−0.5
Discriminability	94	−0.5
Perseveration	5	0.0
Intrusions (*)	7	1.0
Cued-Recall Intrusions (*)	1	0.0
Free-Recall Intrusions (*)	6	1.0

Note: Higher scores are better unless indicated with (*).

G. G.'s List A Total Trials 1–5 was in the impaired range. She was able to recall 3 of 15 words for Trial 1, which was also in the impaired range. This would suggest possible difficulties with auditory attention. As mentioned in Chapter 4, Trial 1 performance should be compared with other auditory working memory tests when possible. Trial 5 was in the low average range, suggesting she benefited from repeated exposure of the words across trials, recalling a maximum of 10 of the 15 words. Her memory for a single presentation of an interference list was in the impaired range as she was able to recall only 3 of the 15 words from this new list. This is consistent with her recall of the initial presentation of list A and further suggests that she has difficulties with auditory attention. Additionally, she demonstrated a slight primacy effect with more words recalled from the beginning of the list relative to the middle and end.

Short-delayed free recall was a raw score of 10, with recall of the same words from the last presentation of the original list. At long-delay free recall, her retention of the original list was diminished from 10 words to 7 words, which was 1.5 standard deviations below the mean, suggesting a weakness for delayed recall of verbal information. In general, her long-delay cued recall was better than her long-delay free recall. Taken together, this pattern of results suggests that she is able to retain information but has difficulties with retrieval in the absence of cues. Her recognition of the original list of words was in the average range (11 of 15), which further suggests that her memory difficulties lie in her ability to retrieve, as opposed to retain, information. In general, these results indicate that G. G. experienced information organization and retrieval difficulties but benefited from memory enhancing techniques like repetition of information and contextual cues.

Results from this assessment supported a diagnosis of post-concussion syndrome. Recommendations made based on the findings from the CVLT-C included initiating a 504 plan at school to help support her academics with the following accommodations: (a) class slides and notes provided ahead of time and/or access to another student's notes or a lecture outline as a supplement to her class notes; (b) when possible, tests and quizzes presented in multiple-choice format as opposed to short or long essay format; (c) preferential seating at the front of the class; and (d) Break down tasks into smaller, more manageable pieces with intermediate due dates before the final due date. Based on the results of the CVLT-C and other memory testing, the following memory specific recommendations were provided. Taking frequent breaks when completing cognitively demanding tasks such as homework. For example, working for 45 min and taking a 10-min break before resuming work. Developing a multisensory approach to learning new information was recommended including (a) utilizing Venn diagrams to help understand the relationships between concepts, (b) utilizing mind maps to help link information and concepts in lessons to one another, and (c) creating verbal and/or visual mnemonics to cluster information together.

CONCLUSION

The cases presented in this chapter represent only a fraction of the types of cases and scenarios where the CVLT might be utilized. At times, a distinct and expected pattern of test performance emerges and at other times testing is much better or much worse than expected. Accurate interpretation of the CVLT takes practice, starting with a few basic scores and then taking a more thorough look at process scores in the context of other clinical data is an efficient approach to interpreting data. Chapter 4 of this text provides more details on the interpretation of the CVLT and Chapter 6 provides a discussion of literature findings on CVLT performance within various clinical populations.

References

Acharya, S., Wu, S., Ashford, J. M., Tinkle, C. L., Lucas, J. T., Qaddoumi, I., ... Merchant, T. E. (2019). Association between hippocampal dose and memory in survivors of childhood or adolescent low-grade glioma: A 10-year neurocognitive longitudinal study. *Neuro-Oncology*, *21*(9), 1175–1183.

Armstrong, N. M., An, Y., Ferrucci, L., Deal, J. A., Lin, F. R., & Resnick, S. M. (2018). Temporal sequence of hearing impairment and cognition in the Baltimore Longitudinal Study of Aging. *Journals of Gerontology: Medical Sciences*, 1–7. doi:10.1093/gerona/gly268

Baker, D. A., Connery, A. K., Kirk, J. W., & Kirkwood, M. W. (2014). Embedded performance validity indicators within the California Verbal Learning Test, Children's Version. *The Clinical Neuropsychologist*, *28*, 116–127.

Bauer, L., Yantz, C. L., Ryan, L. M., Warden, D. L., & McCaffrey, R. J. (2005). An examination of the California Verbal Learning Test II to detect incomplete effort in a traumatic brain-injury sample. *Applied Neuropsychology*, *12*, 202–207.

Bellugi, U., Bihrle, A., Neville, H., Doherty, S., & Jernigan, T. (1992). Language, cognition, and brain organization in a neurodevelopmental disorder. In M. R. Gunnar & C. A. Nelson (Eds.), *Developmental behavioral neuroscience: The Minnesota symposia on child psychology* (Vol. *24*, pp. 201–232). Hillsdale, NJ: Erlbaum.

Benedict, R. H. B., Schretlen, D., Groninger, L., & Brandt, J. (1998). Hopkins Verbal Learning Test - Revised: Normative data and analysis of inter-form and test-retest reliability. *The Clinical Neuropsychologist*, *12*, 43–55.

Bercaw, E. L., Hanks, R. A., Millis, S. R., & Gola, T. J. (2011). Changes in neuropsychological performance after traumatic brain injury from inpatient rehabilitation to 1-year follow-up in predicting 2-year functional outcomes. *The Clinical Neuropsychologist*, *25*(1), 72–89.

Bilgel, M., An, Y., Lang, A., Prince, J., Ferrucci, L., Jedynak, B., & Resnick, S. M. (2014). Trajectories of Alzheimer disease-related cognitive measures in a longitudinal sample. *Alzheimer's & Dementia*, *10*(6), 735–742.

Brazo, P., Ilongo, M., & Dollfus, S. (2013). Distinct episodic verbal memory profiles in schizophrenia. *Behavioral Science*, *3*(2), 192–205.

Brønnick, K., Alves, G., Aarsland, D., Tysnes, O. B., & Larsen, J. P. (2011). Verbal memory in drug-naive, newly diagnosed Parkinson's disease. The retrieval deficit hypothesis revisited. *Neuropsychology*, *25*(1), 114–124.

Brooks, B. L., & Ploetz, D. M. (2015). Embedded performance validity on the CVLT-C for youth with neurological disorders. *Archives of Clinical Neuropsychology*, *30*, 200–206.

Brooks, B. L., Ploetz, D. M., & Kirkwood, M. W. (2016). A survey of neuropsychologists' use of validity tests with children and adolescents. *Archives of Clinical Neuropsychology*, *27*, 23–29.

Bush, S., Heilbronner, R., & Ruff, R. (2014). Psychological assessment of symptom and performance validity, response bias, and malingering: Official position of the Association for Scientific Advancement in Psychological Injury and Law. *Psychological Injury and Law*, *7*, 197–205.

Camicioli, R. M., Korzan, J. R., Foster, S. L., Fisher, N. J., Emery, D. J., Bastos, A. C., & Hanstock, C. C. (2004). Posterior cingulate metabolic changes occur in Parkinson's disease patients without dementia. *Neuroscience Letters*, *354*(3), 177–180.

Cohen, M. (1997). *Children's Memory Scale*. San Antonio, TX: The Psychological Corporation.

Corbett, L., Karyadi, K. A., Kinney, D., Nitch, S. R., Bayan, S. M., & Williams, M. (2018). Impaired verbal learning in forensic inpatients with schizophrenia spectrum disorder. *Applied Neuropsychology. Adult*, *25*(3), 189–196.

Costers, L., Gielen, J., Eelen, P. L., Van Schependom, J., Laton, J., Van Remoortel, A., et al. (2017). Does including the full CVLT-II and BVMT-R improve BICAMS? Evidence from a Belgian (Dutch) validation study. *Multiple Sclerosis and Related Disorders*, *18*, 33–40.

Cutting, L. E., Koth, C. W., Mahone, E. M., & Denckla, M. B. (2003). Evidence for unexpected weaknesses in learning in children with attention-deficit/hyperactivity disorder without reading disabilities. *Journal of Learning Disabilities*, *36*(3), 259–269.

Delis, D. C., Cullum, C. M., Butters, N., Cairns, P., & Prifitera, A. (1988). Wechsler memory scale-revised and California verbal learning test: Convergence and divergence. *The Clinical Neuropsychologist*, *2*(2), 188–196.

Delis, D. C., Fine, E. M., Stricker, J. L., Houston, W. S., Wetter, S. R., Cobell, K., ... & Bondi, M. W. (2010). Comparison of the traditional recall-based versus a new list-based method for computing semantic clustering on the California Verbal Learning Test: Evidence from Alzheimer's disease. *The Clinical Neuropsychologist*, *24*(1), 70–79.

Delis, D. C., Freeland, J., Kramer, J. H., & Kaplan, E. (1988). Integrating clinical assessment with cognitive neuroscience: Construct validation of the California Verbal Learning Test. *Journal of Consulting and Clinical Psychology*, *56*(1), 123.

Delis, D. C., Kaplan, E., & Kramer, J. H. (2001). *Delis-Kaplan executive function system*. Bloomington, MN: Pearson.

Delis, D. C., Kramer, J. H., Kaplan, E., & Ober, B. A. (1987). *California Verbal Learning Test*. San Antonio, TX: The Psychological Corporation.

Delis, D. C., Kramer, J. H., Kaplan, E., & Ober, B. A. (1994). *California Verbal Learning Test - Children's Version*. San Antonio, TX: NCS Pearson.

Delis, D. C., Kramer, J. H., Kaplan, E., & Ober, B. A. (2000). *California Verbal Learning Test* (2nd ed.). San Antonio, TX: NCS Pearson.

Delis, D. C., Kramer, J. H., Kaplan, E., & Ober, B. A. (2017). *California Verbal Learning Test* (3rd ed.). San Antonio, TX: NCS Pearson.

Delis, D. C., Wetter, S. R., Jacobson, M. W., Peavy, G., Hamilton, J., Gongvatana, A., ... & Salmon, D. P. (2005). Recall discriminability: Utility of a new CVLT–II measure in the differential diagnosis of dementia. *Journal of the International Neuropsychological Society*, *11*(6), 708–715.

Di Pinto, M., Conklin, H. M., Li, C., & Merchant, T. E. (2012). Learning and memory following conformal radiation therapy for pediatric craniopharyngioma and low-grade glioma. *International Journal of Radiation Oncology, Biology, Physics*, *84*(3), e363–e369.

Di Pinto, M., Conklin, H. M., Li, C., Xiong, X., & Merchant, T. E. (2010). Investigating verbal and visual auditory learning after conformal radiation therapy for childhood ependymoma. *International Journal of Radiation Oncology, Biology, Physics*, *77*(4), 1002–1008.

Donders, J., & Minnema, M. T. (2004). Performance discrepancies on the California Verbal Learning Test-Children's Vversion (CVLT-C) in children with traumatic brain injury. *Journal of International Neuropsychological Society*, *10*(4), 482–488.

Donders, J., & Nienhuis, J. B. (2007). Utility of California Verbal Learning Test, recall discriminability indices in the evaluation of traumatic brain injury. *Journal of the International Neuropsychological Society*, *13*(2), 354–358.

Duinmeijer, I., de Jong, J., & Scheper, A. (2012). Narrative abilities, memory and attention in children with a specific language impairment. *International Journal of Language & Communication Disorders*, *47*(5), 542–555.

Ebbinghaus, H. (1885). Memory: A contribution to experimental psychology. Reprinted in 2013. *Annals of Neurosciences*, *20*, 155–156.

Edelstein, B. A., & Koven, L. (2011). Older adult assessment issues and strategies. In V. Molinari (Ed.), *Specialty competencies in geropsychology* (pp. 41–57). Oxford, NY: Oxford University Press.

Elderkin-Thompson, V., Mintz, J., Haroon, E., Lavretsky, H., & Kumar, A. (2007). Executive dysfunction and memory in older patients with major and minor depression. *Archives of Clinical Neuropsychology*, *22*(2), 261–270.

Filoteo, J. V., Salmon, D. P., Schiehser, D. M., Kane, A. E., Hamilton, J. M., Rilling, L. M., … & Galasko, D. R. (2009). Verbal learning and memory in patients with dementia with Lewy bodies or Parkinson's disease with dementia. *Journal of Clinical and Experimental Neuropsychology, 31*(7), 823–834.

Fisher, N. J., & DeLuca, J. W. (1997). Verbal learning strategies of adolescents and adults with the syndrome of nonverbal learning disabilities. *Child Neuropsychology, 3*(3), 192–198.

Fiszdon, J. M., Silverstein, S. M., Buchwald, J., Hull, J. W., & Smith, T. E. (2003). Verbal memory in schizophrenia: Sex differences over repeated assessments. *Schizophrenia Research, 61*(2–3), 235–243.

Foldi, N. S., Brickman, A. M., Schaefer, L. A., & Knutelska, M. E. (2003). Distinct serial position profiles and neuropsychological measures differentiate late life depression from normal aging and Alzheimer's disease. *Psychiatry Research, 120*(1), 71–84.

Godfrey, M., & Lee, N. R. (2018). Memory profiles in Down syndrome across development: A review of memory abilities through the lifespan. *Journal of Neurodevelopmental Disorders, 10*(1), 5.

Goldberg, T. E., Harvey, P. D., Wesnes, K. A., Snyder, P. J., & Schneider, L. S. (2015). Practice effects due to serial cognitive assessment: Implications for preclinical Alzheimer's disease randomized controlled trials. *Alzheimer's & Dementia: Diagnosis, Assessment & Disease Monitoring, 1*, 103–111.

Graves, L. V., Drozdick, L., Courville, T., Farrer, T. J., Gilbert, P. E., & Delis, D. C. (2019). Cohort differences on the CVLT-II and CVLT3: evidence of a negative Flynn effect on the attention/working memory and learning trials. *The Clinical neuropsychologist*, 1–18. Advance online publication. doi:10.1080/13854046.2019.1699605

Graves, L. V., Holden, H. M., Van Etten, E. J., Delano-Wood, L., Bondi, M. W., Salmon, D. P., … & Delis, D. C. (2019). New intrusion analyses on the CVLT-3: Utility in distinguishing the memory disorders of Alzheimer's versus Huntington's disease. *Journal of the International Neuropsychological Society, 25*(8), 878–883.

Hamilton, J. M., Salmon, D. P., Galasko, D., Delis, D. C., Hansen, L. A., Masliah, E., … & Thal, L.J. (2004). A comparison of episodic memory deficits in neuropathologically-confirmed Dementia with Lewy bodies and Alzheimer's disease. *Journal of the International Neuropsychological Society, 10*(5), 689–697.

Heilbronner, R. L., Sweet, J. J., Morgan, J. E., Larrabee, G. J., & Millis, S. R., & Conference Participants (2009). American Academy of Clinical Neuropsychology consensus conference statement on the neuropsychological assessment of effort, response bias, and malingering. *The Clinical Neuropsychologist, 23*, 1093–1129.

Higginson, C. I., Wheelock, V. L., Carroll, K. E., & Sigvardt, K. A. (2005). Recognition memory in Parkinson's disease with and without dementia: Evidence inconsistent with the retrieval deficit hypothesis. *Journal of Clinical and Experimental Neuropsychology, 27*(4), 516–528.

Hill, S. K., Beers, S. R., Kmiec, J. A., Keshavan, M. S., & Sweeney, J. A. (2004). Impairment of verbal memory and learning in antipsychotic-naıve patients with first-episode schizophrenia. *Schizophrenia Research, 68*(2–3), 127–136.

Hoff, A. L., Svetina, C., Shields, G., Stewart, J., & DeLisi, L. E. (2005). Ten year longitudinal study of neuropsychological functioning subsequent to a first episode of schizophrenia. *Schizophrenia Research, 78*(1), 27–34.

Holcomb, M. J. (2018). Pediatric performance validity testing: State of the field and current research. *Journal of Pediatric Neuropsychology, 4*, 83–85.

Huh, T. J., Kramer, J. H., Gazzaley, A., & Delis, D. C. (2006). Response bias and aging on a recognition memory task. *Journal of the International Neuropsychological Society, 12*(1), 1–7.

Hutchens, R. L., Kinsella, G. J., Ong, B., Pike, K. E., Parsons, S., Storey, E., … & Clare, L. (2012). Knowledge and use of memory strategies in amnestic mild cognitive impairment. *Psychology and Aging, 27*(3), 768–777.

Jacobs, M. L., & Donders, J. (2007). Criterion validity of the California Verbal Learning Test-(CVLT-II) after traumatic brain injury. *Archives of Clinical Neuropsychology, 22*(2), 143–149.

Kaplan, E. (1988). A process approach to neuropsychological assessment. In T. Boll & B. K. Bryant (Eds.), *Clinical neuropsychology and brain function: Research, measurement, and practice* (pp. 125–167). Washington, DC: American Psychological Corporation.

Kibby, M. Y. (2009). Memory functioning in developmental dyslexia: An analysis using two clinical memory measures. *Archives of Clinical Neuropsychology, 24*(3), 245–254.

Korkman, M., Kirk, U., & Kemp, S. (2007). *NEPSY* (2nd ed.). Bloomington, MN: Pearson NCS.

Kramer, J. H., & Delis, D. C. (1991). Interference effects on the California Verbal Learning Test: A construct validation study. *Psychological Assessment: A Journal of Consulting and Clinical Psychology, 3*(2), 299.

Kramer, J. H., Delis, D. C., Kaplan, E., O'Donnell, L., & Prifitera, A. (1997). Developmental sex differences in verbal learning. *Neuropsychology, 11*, 577–584.

Kramer, J. H., Knee, K., & Delis, D. C. (2000). Verbal memory impairments in dyslexia. *Archives of Clinical Neuropsychology, 15*(1), 83–93.

Lee, S., Ong, B., Pike, K. E., Mullaly, E., Rand, E., Storey, E., . . . & Kinsella, G. J. (2016). The contribution of prospective memory performance to the neuropsychological assessment of mild cognitive impairment. *The Clinical Neuropsychologist, 30*(1), 131–149.

Lezak, M. D., Howieson, D. B., Bigler, E. D., & Tranel, D. (2012). *Neuropsychological assessment* (5th ed.). New York, NY: Oxford University Press.

Libon, D. J., Swenson, R., Ashendorf, L., Bauer, R. M., & Bowers, D. (2013). Edith Kaplan and the boston process approach. *The Clinical Neuropsychologist, 27*, 1223–1233.

Lichtenberg, P. A., Mast, B. T., Carpenter, B. D., & Wetherell, J. (2015). *APA handbook of clinical geropsychology, vol. 2: Assessment, treatment, and issues of later life*. Washington, DC: American Psychological Association.

Lichtenstein, J. D., Erdodi, L. A., & Linnea, K. S. (2017). Introducing a forced-choice recognition task to the California Verbal Learning Test - Children's Version. *Child Neuropsychology, 23*, 284–299. doi:10.1080/09297049.2015.1135422

Lichtenstein, J. D., Holcomb, M., & Erdodi, L. A. (2018). One-minute PVT: Further evidence for the utility of the California Verbal Learning Test - children's Version forced choice recognition trial. *Journal of Pediatric Neuropsychology, 4*, 94–104.

Lundervold, A. J., Wollschläger, D., & Wehling, E. (2014). Age and sex related changes in episodic memory function in middle aged and older adults. *Scandinavian Journal of Psychology, 55*(3), 225–232.

Martin, P. K., Schroeder, R. W., & Odland, A. P. (2015). Neuropsychologists' validity testing beliefs and practices: A survey of North American professionals. *The Clinical Neuropsychologists*, (6), 741–776.

McLaughlin, P. M., Wright, M. J., LaRocca, M., Nguyen, P. T., Teng, E., Apostolova, L. G., . . . & Woo, E. (2014). The "Alzheimer's type" profile of semantic clustering in amnestic mild cognitive impairment. *Journal of the International Neuropsychological Society, 20*(4), 402–412.

Mesholam-Gately, R. I., Giuliano, A. J., Zillmer, E. A., Barakat, L. P., Kumar, A., Gur, R. C., . . . & Moberg, P. J. (2012). Verbal learning and memory in older adults with minor and major depression. *Archives of Clinical Neuropsychology, 27*(2), 196–207.

Mitrushina, M., Boone, K. B., Razani, J., & D'Elia, L. F. (2005). *Handbook of normative data for neuropsychological assessment*. New York, NY: Oxford University Press.

Mottram, L., & Donders, J. (2006). Cluster subtypes on the California Verbal Learning Test - Children's Version after pediatric traumatic brain injury. *Developmental Neuropsychology, 30*(3), 865–883.

Muir-Broaddus, J. E., Rosenstein, L. D., Medina, D. E., & Soderberg, C. (2002). Neuropsychological test performance of children with ADHD relative to test norms and parent behavioral ratings. *Archives of Clinical Neuropsychology, 17*(7), 671–689.

Nichols, S., Jones, W., Roman, M. J., Wulfeck, B., Delis, D. C., Reilly, J., & Bellugi, U. (2004). Mechanisms of verbal memory impairment in four neurodevelopmental disorders. *Brain and Language, 88*(2), 180–189.

Ogletree, B. T. (1998). Test review of California Verbal Learning Test, Children's Version. In J. C. Impara & B. S. Plake (Eds.), *The thirteenth mental measurements yearbook*. Lincoln: University of

Nebraska Press. Retrieved from http://marketplace.unl.edu/buros/ *Archives of Clinical Neuropsychology, 11*, 171–173.

Osterrieth, P. A. (1944). Filetest de copie d'une figure complex: Contribution a l'etude de la perception et de la memoire [The test of copying a complex figure: A contribution to the study of perception and memory]. *Archives de Psychologie, 30*, 286–356.

Paolo, A. M., Troster, A. I., & Ryan, J. J. (1997). California Verbal Learning Test: Normative data for the elderly. *Journal of Clinical and Experimental Neuropsychology, 2*, 220–234.

Parikh, M., Hynan, L. S., Weiner, M. F., Lacritz, L., Ringe, W., & Cullum, C. M. (2014). Single neuropsychological test scores associated with rate of cognitive decline in early Alzheimer disease. *The Clinical Neuropsychologist, 28*(6), 926–940.

Pearson. (2009). *Advanced clinical solutions for WAIS-IV and WMS-IV*. San Antonio, TX: Author.

Pike, K. E., Rowe, C. C., Moss, S. A., & Savage, G. (2008). Memory profiling with paired associate learning in Alzheimer's disease, mild cognitive impairment, and healthy aging. *Neuropsychology, 22*(6), 718–728.

Poreh, A. M., Avital, R., Dines, P. L., & Levin, J. B. (2015). The effects of age of language acquisition on verbal memory tests in a sample of older adults immigrants. *Psychology & Neuroscience, 8*, 66–74.

Pozueta, A., Rodríguez-Rodríguez, E., Vazquez-Higuera, J. L., Mateo, I., Sánchez-Juan, P., González-Perez, S., ... & Combarros, O. (2011). Detection of early Alzheimer's disease in MCI patients by the combination of MMSE and an episodic memory test. *BMC Neurology, 11*(1), 78.

Rabin, L. A., Paré, N., Saykin, A. J., Brown, M. J., Wishart, H. A., Flashman, L. A., & Santulli, R. B. (2009). Differential memory test sensitivity for diagnosing amnestic mild cognitive impairment and predicting conversion to Alzheimer's disease. *Aging, Neuropsychology, and Cognition, 16*(3), 357–376.

Ragland, J. D., Coleman, A. R., Gur, R. C., Glahn, D. C., & Gur, R. E. (2000). Sex differences in brain-behavior relationships between verbal episodic memory and resting regional cerebral blood flow. *Neuropsychologia, 38*(4), 451–461.

Rey, A. (1941). "L'examen psychologique dans les cas d'encephalopathie traumatique.(Les problems.)." *Archives de Psychologie, 28*, 215–285.

Rund, B. R., Barder, H. E., Evensen, J., Haahr, U., Hegelstad, W. T. V., Joa, I., ... & Opjordsmoen, S. (2015). Neurocognition and duration of psychosis: A 10-year follow-up of first-episode patients. *Schizophrenia Bulletin, 42*(1), 87–95.

Salthouse, T. A. (1996). General and specific speed mediation of adult age differences in memory. *The Journals of Gerontology: Series B, 51B*, P30–P42.

Salvia, J., Ysseldyke, J., & Bolt, S. (2013). *Assessment in special and inclusive education* (12th ed.). Belmont, CA: Wadsworth.

Schmidt, M. (1996). *Rey Auditory Verbal Learning Test*. Torrance, CA: WPS.

Shear, P. K., Tallal, P., & Delis, D. C. (1992). Verbal learning and memory in language impaired children. *Neuropsychologia, 30*(5), 451–458.

Sheslow, D., & Adams, W. (2003). *Wide range assessment of memory and learning* (2nd ed.). Bloomington, MN: Pearson.

Shura, R. D., Miskey, H. M., Rowland, J. A., Yoash-Gantz, R. E., & Denning, J. H. (2016). Embedded performance validity measures with postdeployment veterans: Cross-validation and efficiency with multiple measures. *Applied Neuropsychology. Adult, 23*, 94–104.

Silva, D., Guerreiro, M., Maroco, J., Santana, I., Rodrigues, A., Marques, J. B., & de Mendonça, A. (2012). Comparison of four verbal memory tests for the diagnosis and predictive value of mild cognitive impairment. *Dementia and Geriatric Cognitive Disorders Extra, 2*(1), 120–131.

Smith, G. E., & Bondi, M. W. (2013). *Mild cognitive impairment and dementia: Definitions, diagnosis, and treatment*. New York, NY: Oxford University Press.

Stratton, J., Cobia, D. J., Reilly, J., Brook, M., & Hanlon, R. E. (2018). Differences in neuropsychological functioning between homicidal and nonviolent schizophrenia samples. *Journal of Forensic Sciences, 63*(5), 1435–1443.

Strauss, E., Sherman, E. M. S., & Spreen, O. (2006). *A compendium of neuropsychological tests: Administration, norms, and commentary* (3rd ed.). New York, NY: Oxford University Press.
Sunderaraman, P., Blumen, H. M., DeMatteo, D., Apa, Z., & Cosentino, S. (2013). Task demand influences relationships among sex, clustering strategy, and recall: 16-word versus 9-word list learning tests. *Cognitive and Behavioral Neurology: Official Journal of the Society for Behavioral and Cognitive Neurology, 26*(2), 78–84.
The Psychological Corporation. (1997). *WAIS–III WMS–III technical manual*. San Antonio, TX: The Psychological Corporation.
Tombaugh, T. N. (1996). *The test of memory malingering*. Toronto, Ontario: Multi-Health Systems.
Tromp, D., Dufour, A., Lithfous, S., Pebayle, T., & Després, O. (2015). Episodic memory in normal aging and Alzheimer disease: Insights from imaging and behavioral studies. *Ageing Research Reviews, 24*, 232–262.
Turetsky, B. I., Moberg, P. J., Mozley, L. H., Moelter, S. T., Agrin, R. N., Gur, R. C., & Gur, R. E. (2002). Memory-delineated subtypes of schizophrenia: Relationship to clinical, neuroanatomical, and neurophysiological measures. *Neuropsychology, 16*(4), 481–490.
Turner, A. D., Furey, M. L., Drevets, W. C., Zarate, C., Jr., & Nugent, A. C. (2012). Association between subcortical volumes and verbal memory in unmedicated depressed patients and healthy controls. *Neuropsychologia, 50*(9), 2348–2355.
Tuulio-Henriksson, A., Partonen, T., Suvisaari, J., Haukka, J., & Lönnqvist, J. (2004). Age at onset and cognitive functioning in schizophrenia. *The British Journal of Psychiatry, 185*(3), 215–219.
Van Etten, E. J., Graves, L. V., Taylor, B., Holden, H. M., Lopez, F. V., Williams, M. E., … & Gilbert, P. E. (2019). Recall and recognition discriminability in Parkinson's disease and Huntington's disease. *Journal of Huntington's Disease, 8*(4), 459–465.
Vanderploeg, R. D. (Ed.) (2000). *Clinician's guide to neuropsychological assessment*. Mahwah, NJ: Lawrence Erlbaum Associates Inc.
Vanderploeg, R. D., Curtiss, G., & Belanger, H. G. (2005). Long-term neuropsychological outcomes following mild traumatic brain injury. *Journal of the International Neuropsychological Society, 11*(3), 228–236.
Vanderploeg, R. D., Donnell, A. J., Belanger, H. G., & Curtiss, G. (2014). Consolidation deficits in traumatic brain injury: The core and residual verbal memory defect. *Journal of Clinical and Experimental Neuropsychology, 36*(1), 58–73.
Warschausky, S., Kay, J. B., Chi, P., & Donders, J. (2005). Hierarchical linear modeling of California Verbal Learning Test – Children's Version learning curve characteristics following childhood traumatic head injury. *Neuropsychology, 19*(2), 193–198.
Wechsler, D. (2009). *Wechsler Memory Scale* (4th ed.). Bloomington, MN: Pearson.
Wechsler, D. (2015). *Wechsler Intelligence Scale for Children* (5th ed.). Bloomington, MN: Pearson.
Whiteside, D. M., Gaasedelen, O. J., Hahn-Ketter, A. E., Luu, H., Miller, M. L., Persinger, V., … & Basso, M. R. (2015). Derivation of a cross-domain embedded performance validity measure in a traumatic brain injury. *The Clinical Neuropsychologist, 29*(6), 788–803. doi:10.1080/13854046.2015.1093660
Wiens, A. N., Tindall, A. G., & Crossen, J. R. (1994). California Verbal Learning Test: A normative data study. *The Clinical Neuropsychologist*, (1), 75–90.
Woods, S. P., & Tröster, A. I. (2003). Prodromal frontal/executive dysfunction predicts incident dementia in Parkinson's disease. *Journal of the International Neuropsychological Society, 9*(1), 17–24.
Yeates, K. O., Blumenstein, E., Patterson, C. M., & Delis, D. C. (1995). Verbal learning and memory following pediatric closed-head injury. *Journal of the International Neuropsychological Society, 1*(1), 78–87.
Yoder, M. S., & Turner, T. H. (2014). Assessment via telemental health technology. In S. S. Bush (Ed.), *Psychological assessment of veterans* (pp. 159–167). New York, NY: Oxford University Press.
Zizak, V. S., Filoteo, J. V., Possin, K. L., Lucas, J. A., Rilling, L. M., Davis, J. D., … & Salmon, D. P. (2005). The ubiquity of memory retrieval deficits in patients with frontal-striatal dysfunction. *Cognitive and Behavioral Neurology, 18*(4), 198–205.

Author Index

Subject Index

Printed and bound by CPI Group (UK) Ltd, Croydon, CR0 4YY